"If Only I Knew Then What I Know Now"
WOMEN'S STORIES OF DISCOVERY

Carolyn

Best wishes always !

Lisa Sullivan Bond

"If Only I Knew Then What I Know Now"
WOMEN'S STORIES OF DISCOVERY

Katharine Gilpin • Diane Marie Ford
and Contributors

Front Cover Concept & Design by
Katharine Gilpin & Diane Marie Ford via Canva.com

Overall Cover Design by
Sarah E. Holroyd (sleepingcatbooks.com)

Editing by
Susan Rooks (grammargoddess.com)

ISBN-10: 0998972894
ISBN-13: 978-0-9989728-9-3

Planet of Plentitude Publishing/In Your Own Words
Women Series
First Edition Volume 1
Printed in the United States of America

Planet of Plentitude Publishing
Middleborough, MA

InYourOwnWordsWomen.com

DEDICATION

This collaborative book of women raising their voices is inspired by and dedicated to the spirit and memory of my friend, KD. The power of your voice still echoes as you help to spread the words of women beyond their imaginings. Thank you.

Love, Katharine

Kathleen Dempsey
July 15, 1961 – to August 23, 1992

TABLE OF CONTENTS

Preface

Everyone has a voice. Everyone has something to say. Many choose to remain silent in the belief that their "something to say" is not good enough.

When we put out the call seeking women who wanted to share their very personal stories, we discovered, not surprisingly, that many, although they did not consciously know it, craved and needed a collaborative community environment in which they could safely share. We were moved beyond words by those who did, indeed, step forward.

Born in the 1950s, we were raised by parents of the Greatest Generation, a generation of men who were reluctant to give women the freedom to fully express themselves, let alone fulfill their potential. However, we are not our parents. We are women of the Baby Boomer generation, the generation of peace, love and women's lib! The times they were a changin', as we entered our teens and twenties – it had become somewhat easier for women to begin expressing themselves.

Through decades of soul-searching, self-discovery work, devouring self-help books, classes, training, and education, we began to open up to and accept our own inner beauty and worth. With the support of healing communities, substantive changes took place for each of us. Those changes catapulted us forward to new frontiers.

Our joint collaboration on this, the first book of the In Your Own Words Women Series, was a natural step along the path of liberation and self-expression. The response to our call for women who wanted to share their very personal stories proved that although we "have come a long way, baby," we, as women, still have a long way to go.

We are proud of these women who were courageous enough to not only excavate and re-live their deeply personal and sometimes painful life experiences, but to put them into written words to share their stories with you. The stories written exclusively for *"If Only I Knew Then What I Know Now"* Women's Stories of Discovery were written from a place of vulnerability and courage. The messages are infused with love, hope, insight, hindsight, and healing.

Much of the feedback received from the writers about this undertaking stated it was a revealing and healing process. Some women commented that the writing helped them to move beyond fear or to release their inner child. A common thread was the desire to inspire others to call forth their strength and believe in themselves. Many contributors had never before even considered writing or sharing their stories, let alone having them published. Quite a few were already published authors, but found it uniquely rewarding to be a part of a community of women expressing themselves in such a deep and personal manner.

We hope these stories may serve as a catalyst for you to express yourself, step into your courage, and shine your light. If just one of these stories strikes a chord within you, we urge you to consider being a part of this community and contributing your story in upcoming books in the In Your Own Words Women series. We welcome you to connect with us through InYourOwnWordsWomen.com.

Katharine Gilpin and Diane Marie Ford
April 2018

OUR STORIES

Learning to Love
Stephanie Lee

"Steph, Mom's not responding to me." "What do you mean she's not responding to you?" "I called out to her several times and she's not responding."

My sister and I lived with our mother after both our long-term relationship breakups. That night I was working on my last paper for the quarter for my Master's degree in Kinesiology and Physical Education. I was very annoyed by the interruption as I had so much to do and it was due the next day. And just in case you were wondering, yes, I had waited until the last minute to get it completed.

Over the prior few months, Mom had been complaining about what she called "spells" where she'd get pain in the area of her chest near her tummy. These "spells" came on suddenly and unexpectedly, so it had started to scare my otherwise normally independent mother. She had stopped going places by herself as frequently.

"Well, she'll respond to me," I thought to myself as I walked into her bedroom, with absolute determination.

It was dusk, so I could barely see my mother lying in the center of her king-sized bed. As I flipped the switch on the bedside lamp, light flooded the room and I could see my mother was lifeless and gray. "Wow, they really do turn gray," I thought. My mind reeled as I tried to comprehend the sight before me.

After calling 911 and while I was administering CPR to my mother, I could hear the sirens in the distance. It was comforting to know help was on the way, because even given my determination, my mother was not responding to me.

When the paramedics arrived, they quickly lifted Mom off the bed to put her on the solid floor so they could work on her. Her lightweight nightgown flew up and exposed her naked body underneath, so the paramedics gently but quickly placed her back on the bed and pulled down her nightgown. Later my sister and I mused that if Mom wasn't already dead she would have died of embarrassment knowing all these young men were in her bedroom and saw her naked body. It is so interesting to observe the thoughts you might have in a stressful situation. The paramedics could not revive her.

The coroner had to come to take Mom away. This might sound morbid, but oddly it really wasn't. I sat and talked with my mother while we waited for the coroner. Mom had the most amazingly peaceful look on her face. I said my heartfelt good-byes, feeling we had finally bonded but maybe a little too late. I don't know.

While I was growing up, my mom worked full-time and actively participated in a number of civic and social organizations. There was not a lot of time for her to spend with us at home and saying the words "I love you" was extremely rare. As Mom got older, she started expressing her emotional side more often. The first time she told me she loved me I literally did not know what to say. I was stunned. It was awkward. I said nothing.

One night, not too long before her death, we were watching TV in her bedroom because she had suffered a "spell" earlier that evening. She asked me to come join her and sit on the bed with her. That was something I had always wanted to do with my mother, just like I saw other moms do with their daughters on television shows. But I said no; I was fine in the chair.

Thirty minutes before mom passed away, she was on the phone with some girlfriends planning a potluck luncheon they were to have the next day. Within an hour of her last phone call, she was pronounced dead on the scene.

Days later, before the funeral, I pondered what would have happened if I had simply said "I love you" back when my mother had said it to me that day. How hard was that, really? Even today I wish I could go back and sit on the bed with her while we watched TV together. What I would give to have those moments to do over. But I do not. I only have this moment. Today I tell anyone and everyone, right now, without hesitation, when I feel love for them. I now know the opportunity may not come around again.

That night, over twenty years ago, while I sat and talked with mom, when we were waiting for the coroner, I knew my life had just changed in a very big way. It was a profound change, yet I did not yet comprehend the full impact. I am not even sure I fully comprehend it today.

I offer you this story, with love.

Finding My Voice
Kelley Cabral-Mosher

When did I lose my voice? Was it when my tonsils were taken out at age thirty? Or when I was around four years old and someone "touched" me, and I didn't tell anyone until I was nineteen? Was it when I was coaching and raised my voice in the gym for the girls to hear me? Or was it when my parents were yelling at each other and I couldn't tell them to stop? Was it when I sang so loudly at a concert that the next day my voice was hoarse? Or was it when my brother was stealing from me and it kept happening? Oh, I know; it was when I was laughing so hard with my girlfriends watching the film Bridesmaids that I couldn't get the words out. Or was it when a friend told me I was too sensitive and I stopped sharing?

Maybe it could have been when I was playing basketball and field hockey, yelling with my teammates the next play. Or was it at age fifteen when I was raped in my own bathroom by a neighborhood boy? He covered my mouth – I blacked out, and repressed it until I was in my forties. Was it when I and my sons loudly sang "Living on a Prayer" in the car? Or was it when I asked for alcoholism and addiction not to be around me anymore; yet they were always in my face?

Did I really lose my voice? Or was it that I didn't know I could choose to use it when I wanted or needed to? Well, I did find places where my voice was heard: playing sports, sometimes with my friends, at work, and with my children. Why did I feel my voice was lost? Why have I felt not heard? Why do I feel at times the words are stuck in my throat? I didn't know how and when I needed to use my voice. Maybe it was too painful at the time. Maybe I didn't know what words to use. Maybe I didn't know if anyone really cared to hear it. Maybe I didn't think God or the universe was paying attention to me.

"Your truth is important, little girl." "You can tell them to stop yelling and him to stop stealing." "Your sensitivity is a gift, girlfriend." "You can scream STOP." "Your empathy for recovery is a treasure."

I'm finding my voice again. I'm telling myself now and the "me" from back then – "What I have to say is important, authentic, beautiful, and true."

Here I am – using my beautiful, authentic, important and true voice, to share with you about how I lost it. But – if I hadn't lost it, would I be writing my story – this story, to share with you?

WOMEN'S STORIES OF DISCOVERY

Death Wish
Jennifer Bingham-Maas

Since my twenties I have struggled in an uneasy, dysfunctional relationship with my anger, trying to channel and release it in constructive ways, without ever fully resolving anything. It was a generalized anger; I was "mad" at the world, "mad" at God, and simultaneously conflicted because "good girls" were not permitted to experience, let alone express, such negative emotions as anger, righteous or otherwise, warranted or not.

I was living with my anger, but it was on the periphery, not yet in focus. I gave as much time and attention to it as I felt I could afford, but it wasn't enough. Looking outward for a reason for my anger, it wasn't until I complained to a friend about my recurrent bladder infection that she asked me a simple question, "For what do you need to forgive yourself?" that I was able to shift my focus inward.

The question slipped under my guard; I was momentarily at a loss as I pondered the question. What might I have done or said in anger for which I needed to forgive myself? Almost without conscious awareness, my subconscious brought forth a gift, a memory that I, as an adult, had at one point recalled, analyzed, and dismissed. But I as the inner child had clung to it and still believed, without being aware I continued to perceive it that way. I heard myself saying, "Well, once when I was twelve or so, I was really angry at my mother and I said the most hurtful thing I could think of at the time, which was 'I wish you were dead!' "

Now I know that a lot of pre-teens and teenagers have some of these feelings when they're in conflict with their parents, and that this is not an uncommon sentiment for someone this age. I also feel that I did not come up with this statement on my own and had either read it in a book or seen it in a movie or in an episode on TV or something. I don't recall what incident had sparked the comment, only that I wanted to lash out and inflict as much pain as I could and this would be the clincher. I didn't even really wish it at the time, but it thrilled me in a way to speak so hatefully, while at the same time it scared me, too.

I don't remember how my mother responded – I just recall the electric charge that surged through me as I voiced something that was taboo. I probably wouldn't have given it another thought if my malevolent wish hadn't been fulfilled two years later. My logical adult self realizes that by saying it I didn't actually cause my mother's death. But my twelve-year-old self, from her egocentric perspective, absolutely believes in magical thinking and that there is a direct correlation between that "wish" and my mother's death.

It was the lack of self-control and resulting destructive anger that converged to make manifest my idle wish, ending a chapter in my life. I had never forgiven myself. I directed that anger inward, punishing myself for causing my mother's death, taking responsibility for having wished it, and blaming God for taking me at my word and fulfilling my wish... the power of words and the scars they can leave.

Words do have the power to hurt. While such wounds may not be obvious, not in the way a physical beating can be easily seen by bruises or broken bones, they tend, without being questioned, to be internalized into the subconscious where they become part of your shadow. This happens easily, especially in childhood, when your ability to consider the source or to gain perspective, or even to be mindful as to how to process the information has yet to develop. You can get caught up in the emotions evoked by the words.

Bruises and broken bones eventually heal, whereas a careless word or thought often festers in the dark of the unconscious, leaving the wound as fresh as the moment it occurred. Like the eyes on a sprouting potato in a root cellar, the words, when triggered by something, take on a life of their own as they rise to surface.

I wish I knew then what I know now about forgiving myself and having compassion for that twelve-year-old girl who lost far more than her temper. By bringing her pain and suffering into consciousness and reassuring her that she has been forgiven – that indeed, there is nothing to forgive – she can release the anger and begin to heal. As she forgives herself, she can stop punishing herself for imagined wrongs and can begin again to fully live.

The Importance of Communicating
Nell Conway

On an average day, our mailbox is full of coupons, credit card offers, and circulars – so many junk mail offers that at times we forget about personal correspondence. When I arrived home on a dark November evening to a handwritten, small blue envelope, I was happily surprised.

Growing up in the 1990s and 2000s, technology was a huge part of my life. At ten years old, I began communicating with friends through online instant messaging. I could sit home on any day of the week and connect with hundreds of people all over the world. Technology led us all to believe we were building connections with the important people in our lives.

As I continued my journey through life, I had the great fortune to travel around the world. From

Australia, Israel, to South America and a road trip around the states, I met a wide array of fascinating people. After making a new friend, I always relied on the power of technology to keep connected and build a friendship.

But I soon learned that real friendships are based on more than just a "like" or comment on Facebook. Over the years I have lost valuable friendships by my lack of human connection. Technology was not enough to withstand the stress of time and distance on a relationship.

Now that I am thirty years old, I feel at times more of a bystander than part of the group. I witness much of life through my Wi-Fi connection, on-screen vs. in person. So many friends are getting married and having children, yet so many lives are disconnected while actually being connected like never before.

So when that small blue envelope arrived, it provided me with the simple reminder I needed. Inside the envelope was a simple note from a new friend, sharing what a pleasure it was to have met me.

Make no mistake: I have built a career on the power of technology; born, bred, and adapted my life to it, in fact. However, to truly build and maintain friendships, it is now as it has always been: the power of a personal note, a simple phone call, the semblance of personal interaction, or even the power of a handshake that allows these relationships to meet the test of time. And if I knew then what I know now, I would have communicated with every wonderful person I had met on a personal level beyond just the click of a button.

WOMEN'S STORIES OF DISCOVERY

Unbroken Beauty
Lisa Sinkiewicz

If only I knew then what I know now... a single moment in time would forever change who I am. A moment would change my heart and soul so deeply that the ripple of its pain would resonate, utterly shaking me to my core, even years later when the thought of that moment lay dormant

If I had only known it wasn't dormant.

May 7, 1992... I awoke that morning to a bright, soft sunlight, a mere week before turning fifteen, to experience the day as no other before or to come. Unsuspecting, I moved through the hours as I had days and weeks and months before. In a single moment, the known turned on me, becoming a vile, hated stranger who stole innocence and life from my body and soul. A trusted coward exerted power to take what was not his in that moment – or ever –

stripping from me the life and vigor with which I entered this world. The spark that could light up a room now flickered, trying to shine despite the heavy breath that often threatened to extinguish it.

RAPE... a word I would despise and not be able to speak. A reality too deep to acknowledge in the hope it would disappear. I desperately yearned to make invisible to my eye and my memory the source of suffering that would lay foundation to years of scarring and layered damage. I consciously lived as if it hadn't happened while it unconsciously took over all of me. It changed me.

My reality... a single moment imprinted on me in unwelcome ways I would feel again and again. My emotions were triggered by the scent of spring, the song that played as he drove me home, and the clock ticking loudly as I counted towards an end. How awful it was to need to rely on a thief to get me home safely when no such thing could ever be achieved after his profound violation.

I would have used my voice had I known then what I know now. I would have fought in that moment to save myself from the need to fight for countless moments afterward. I wouldn't have hidden. I would have faced the anger, pain, and despair I felt. I would have realized I was not to blame, and I had not been ruined. I would have spoken out and leaned in for support. I would have begun the journey of healing then.

Years would pass and time would mark another scar added to this trauma. I questioned this single moment for decades to come. Choices I made and words I spoke attempted to claim power over my life again, but in essence, they only displayed a lack of control so deep it would permeate my heart and soul and deepen the wound that began in that moment. I lived without contemplation, always craving reassurance and affirmation to make up for the worry and second-guessing I experienced daily. Waiting for a man to undo what a man had done, waiting for someone to make me feel undamaged – bitterness, distrust, anger, fear, and desperation consumed my reality… if only I knew then that this was not the way I was meant to survive.

Feelings of not being enough and not being loved became my inner speech – after all, if I had been enough that moment would never have happened. Or so I thought. I lived for years believing I was the reason this happened. Not that I had caused it or done something to deserve it, but rather that I had not been worthy of enough honor and respect for someone to treat me any differently. From that moment on, I was striving to ensure I would never be treated that way again and prove I deserved to move on as if I hadn't been treated that way ever. I never realized that denying acceptance of what happened was the perfect way for this trauma to fester and grow.

If only I knew then what I know now... fighting every situation that made me feel vulnerable, taken advantage of, or powerless, would never change that moment. The fight would never undo what had been done; the fight would only make the effects of that moment more lasting and more deeply rooted. I would have realized long before now that I was a survivor, and I could fight back the moment by accepting it and learning from it, so I could heal and stop the trauma from sinking into every cell of who I am.

I would have realized that no person could ever make this better. No one. I would have realized that despite how I felt in the darkness of that moment, I was never alone. I would have turned to my Creator for healing and trusted what He says about me – I am loved and adored beyond measure. I would have known that we live in a broken world, and I would have been able to forgive. I would have been healed by His will so much sooner. It is in the entirety of my journey that I am able to see the blessings and embrace my unbroken beauty. Knowing all of this now, I accept – what was, what is, and what I know my God says will be.

Pick Up the Pieces
Enna Jimenez

I was the happiest I'd ever been. I would wake up in the morning feeling excited about work, looking forward to my projects, and networking with my friends. I connected with the company culture and its vision, so much so that everywhere I went I talked about how great my company was. My career was growing and more important, I felt like I was making a difference to the bottom-line. I had the best team ever, and I was so proud of all we had accomplished together. Life was great!

"The sky is the limit. Change is good," I always told my team. And I honestly believed those words. Then one day, out of nowhere, everything changed. The company decided to reorganize my department. The brand I had lovingly created and nurtured for many years was stripped away. My responsibilities, along with my staff, reduced to rubble. My position had come full circle. This change rocked and shattered my world, and I felt as if I would never be able to put the pieces back. "Why is this happening?" I asked myself. "Don't they like my work? What did I do wrong? Where did I fail?" But the biggest question that haunted me for months was – "How am I to believe I let them down?" That was the question that tore me up at my core. I didn't quite know how to cope with this. I cried every day at work. I could not focus or concentrate.

My former team rocked; they covered for me. But I was a complete mess. The social butterfly no longer was I. The happy person giving others advice could no longer do so. My family saw it. My kids saw it. I was in bed, just lying there. I couldn't move; couldn't believe this was happening. I cried and cried and cried until there were just no more tears. I beat myself down and kept asking myself "Where did I go wrong?" I honestly didn't know if I would ever be happy again with my career. I hit rock bottom and was the most miserable I had ever been in my entire life, even after going through a divorce.

Thankfully, one day I woke up from this nightmare and told myself, "Enough... enough with this self-pity." I have this plaque that sits at my desk and reads, "If you're handed it, you can handle it." Wow, those words were so true and allowed me to honestly reflect on what I was going through.

I thought I had everything planned; I was going to retire from this company. I still had more to learn on the business side, but I was eager and excited to learn it. For me, the key was surrounding myself with great mentors and coaches, both internally and externally. I was lucky enough to always give of myself selflessly without a thought. I worked hard at building relationships because I truly wanted to get to know people. And these were the folks that picked me up when I was at my lowest. I would have never thought that my colleagues would extend their hands out to me to help me get back up, but they did just that.

Now, it was time for me to take control. I needed to be in charge and decide my future. I needed to decide my fate. And so, I found new light. I found a reason to be happy again. I had a challenge – "Find my

Happiness" again. That was the turning point in my life. Months later, once I had recovered from rock bottom, I found my ground again. I knew where I had to go. I found my purpose.

While it was not an easy path, it was my path. Making the decision to leave the company that I loved so much was bittersweet. Understanding that I still had more to give, more to discover, was my reward. I stayed true to myself and rediscovered my passion. You must be passionate about what you do, and only then will you be fully happy.

Speak My Truth
Diane Marie Ford

My bags were packed, and I was ready to embark upon another journey to yet another workshop in my continued quest for self-discovery. I was seven years sober and oh, so curious and vulnerable. "The answers have to be out there somewhere!"

Although I had peeled back many layers of my "onion" since early sobriety and always questioned my purpose and existence as I came to love and accept myself for all that I am – I struggled with not feeling comfortable in my skin.

From a very young age I had "liked" girls. Yes, I had girl crushes for as far back as I can recall. I did not think there was anything "wrong" with that, until, at the tender age of thirteen, in 1964, when my best friend Patty and I decided to pledge our love by exchanging rings. That afternoon I returned home from school to share my exciting news with my mother. Her response to my announcement was "We'll talk about that when your father comes home."

Talk about "that" we did. My parents told me "girls don't marry girls – they just don't." When I asked them "why?" their response was "they just don't." Without any further explanation, they instructed me to return the ring to Patty. The next day when I handed her the ring, Patty threw it on the floor, stormed away and never spoke to me again. My parents had taken something as pure and simple as a girl crush and turned it into something "wrong and bad." Although I could not make any sense of it, I felt shame and a need to hide how I felt. I started lying to protect myself. A few years later I realized how easy it was to hide my feelings in drugs and alcohol, which I succeeded in doing over the next twenty-seven years.

At age forty-one, in 1992, entering the second year of my sobriety I met the person with whom I knew I would share the rest of my life. I also had the realization that one of the gifts of sobriety was the freedom to tell the truth... rather, the necessity of telling the truth – if I were to remain sober. That same year I "came out" to my family. Although I had uncovered and expressed my truth, I had not yet realized that was another step in my quest for self-discovery.

In June of 1998, I was off to my workshop at Rowe Camp and Conference Center in the tranquil setting of Rowe, Massachusetts, to sit at the feet of my one of my greatest teachers and mentors, Marianne Williamson. There were only seventy-nine of us seeking spiritual nourishment that weekend. We were open to receive and receive we did! The weekend was intimate, raw, holding, enlightening, and so full of love. Taken with the effortlessness with which Marianne conveyed her teachings, I wondered how someone could be so passionate and full of thunder and intention, while being graceful and loving.

I learned many simple lessons that weekend, lessons I had been stepping over all of my life, or not ready to receive – until that weekend. One of the most important lessons was everything I need, I have within. I realize that sounds elementary – but let me tell you, at that time in my life, that moment along my journey, Marianne's messages landed squarely in my heart and soul. I "got it." Up until that weekend I had been searching and searching – always looking outside of myself, when all the while, everything I needed was within. I began a meditation practice to learn how to quiet my ever-curious mind and listen to that still, small voice within. My life continued to unfold and blossom.

Six years later, after resigning from corporate America, I founded my own company and chose Listen To Thyself as the name, because of its profound simplicity. Each day provided, and to this day continues to provide, new opportunities for me to speak my truth and stand in my power with thunder and passion. I savor the gifts of sobriety and self-expression, step by step, day by day.

It has been twenty-six years since I made the decision to speak my truth and "come out" to my family. I have traveled quite a distance, spiritually and emotionally. Though the journey has tested me and continues to challenge me, I could not have traveled this distance alone.

In reflection, I know I would never have had the courage to say what I needed to say, or to be who I was dying to be, without support, without my teachers and mentors, and the lessons they were (are) compelled to share.

Today I live in freedom unlike I have ever lived in my sixty-six years because I am free to be who I am and express my feelings. I no longer feel the need to hide. Oh, trust me, it didn't happen overnight and I didn't accomplish it by myself. It took courage, self-love, encouragement, support, belief, and a community of like-minded loving people who believed in me enough to take a stand for and bring out the best in me.

Get the Crayons Back
Stephanie Borden

When I was three years old, I had eye surgery to correct Strabismus, also known as crossed eyes. As a child of the sixties I was lovingly compared to Clarence the Cross-Eyed Lion.

I remember so much about the whole experience. I clearly recall dropping my brothers off at my grandfather's house, so he could watch them while my parents took me to the hospital. I can still remember that I wore my white straw Easter bonnet and navy-blue Easter coat to the hospital, and I was so frustrated by the little girl in the next bed because she only spoke French. I received the newest doll on the market from my parents to keep me company, Little Miss No Name, with the plastic tear on her cheek.

It was during the hospital stay that I had my first recollection of being truly paralyzed by what I now know was a completely irrational fear. A few days after surgery, I was placed in the bedside chair with crayons, a coloring book, and a call button to press if I needed anything. To ensure my safety, I was tied to the chair with a restraint that went across my chest. I recall feeling quite pleased at being allowed out of bed and having a new box of crayons. New crayons are always a bit more special than used ones. The box of crayons slipped off my lap onto to the floor and because of the restraint I couldn't reach them. I so vividly recall being absolutely terrified of pushing the call button to get help. I just couldn't do it. So, I simply sat in the chair with the one crayon I had, waiting for the nurse to come back into the room.

Though that happened a very long time ago, I can still feel the clutching fear that stopped me from taking the action I knew would bring me happiness: getting the crayons back! I was so young, what could I possibly have been afraid of?

How many times throughout my life had I let that same "grab me in the chest," "steal my breath," cold, or greasy fear stop me from taking the action that I knew or hoped was the right thing for me to do?

It was Franklin Delano Roosevelt who said, "The only thing we have to fear is fear itself." If only I had only known the truth of those words.

How is it I could see how others were preventing themselves from moving forward or making a change because they let fear stop them, yet I often let fear stop me? As I learned the power of trusting my own instincts and questioning what there really was to be afraid of, it became easier to acknowledge the fear, and then be brave enough to take action. As with most things in life, each time I pushed myself to accept the fear, but didn't let it stop me, I realized a huge sense of accomplishment, no matter the outcome.

I now ask myself when faced with fear, what's the worst thing that could happen?

The Choice
Lau Lapides

Hush – Hurry up – Decide NOW! We were not supposed to talk about it. We were not supposed to be there. It was taboo. As we sat anxiously awaiting our turn to be called into the room, a million thoughts swirled in our heads. We were tired, stressed, and scared. As we sat in the hot, damp, dark hallway, we felt beads of sweat dripping down our necks, our backs, and our palms. Feeling the wetness seep into the carefully placed, crisp bills strapped to our backs and bellies and stuffed in our shoes, we worried the bills would become moist or crinkled and become unusable. Would they need to be replaced? We were in a Ukrainian orphanage – a baby home. It felt like purgatory waiting for him – the stranger.

Jeremy, my sturdy, steadfast husband of five years and father-to-be, sat quietly in his thoughts. Every wrinkle on his forehead forecast terror. Waiting for the little boy while sitting in the back seat of the speeding SUV, we eagerly and hurriedly said "OK" to our lawyer, Sergay. Sergay retorted, "He's perfect, don't worry. You Americans treat everything like it's a TV set! He's not a TV. He's a human being and he's perfect!"

Next a shakedown in the middle of the night to move as quickly as possible, as time is money and someone else might take him. A ten-hour drive to the Crimea with our Sherpa leading the way, loaded with cigarettes, coffee, and Red Bull, so fast and so immediate to make this lifelong decision. "That's the way it's done if you're serious!"

Through the vast endless miles of yellow sunflower fields and burning heat, we encountered old women in head wraps selling onions and watermelons on the corner, and blockades of men in uniforms speaking gibberish: demanding money or threatening to jail our brave leader. After our "OK," we were to say nothing else.

With no time to rest, or change clothing, or even think about why we were sitting in this hallway, we watched tall women in white swiftly move through their rounds, pushing small tables of supplies, instruments, and food. In a seemingly alien tongue, they gazed at us, excitedly squealing, "Seorgy!" Everyone in the orphanage knew, all of the Crimea knew, Ukraine and the government knew, even the children knew. We were Americans with money and no child. And we were coming to take one of theirs. We were strangers in a strange land and we didn't belong; we were outsiders, invaders.

I asked myself if I was awake, if this was real. My heart and my soul opened for a moment; I took a breath. Am I ready to accept this toddler, this little foreigner, to merge and bond, love and protect forever? My senses came alive; I smelled the perfume of detergent, perspiration, desperation, old cookies, hidden Cheerios, vitamins, and determination. I felt I might vomit. "Drink water," Jeremy said, "It will be OK." I wanted to run home. I wanted fresh air and freedom from this choice. I wanted to run and pretend this was not happening. I wanted to erase this choice from our lives and start again. I bargained with God: if He would let me off the hook and bring me back to a year ago when I was open and free, recklessly impulsive and selfish, I would do anything, give Him anything, pay the price for my mistake.

As Sergay led us into the room I realized there was no backing out. We sat on the old leather sofa and wearily gazed at the handsome man with kind eyes behind the desk named "Director." He asked us questions and we answered them, our lawyer interpreting every word to the best of his ability. He showed us government documents of the biological parents and gave us minimal information: he was a taxi driver; she was thirty-eight, Christian Orthodox, unmarried and poor. It would be a "sin" to keep this child, so they gave him up at two days old. She looked like me, Jeremy still tells everyone – even to this day.

"Director" was the arbiter, the oracle for the little ones who had no face, no name, and no identity. He protected the forgotten and the unknowns coming from hidden places and hidden people. He was the advocate, the father, the superhero of these souls who came from the shadows, the underground.

A woman in white with a tired smile entered, holding the hand of this toddler. He quietly stood like a mannequin, stiff with fear, wearing mismatched American-style clothing, yellow tights and old shoes. It was stifling hot and the tears were wet on his face. He couldn't breathe due to congestion, illness, lack of nutrition, and the need for a place to belong. He was placed in my arms like an oversized baby with legs hanging down, and arms around my neck choking me. He squeezed and desperately clung on for fear of drowning, of being let go and forgotten again.

While in Ukraine we were urged never to speak of this transaction, the adoption, the money exchange, or "gifts" to the judges, lawyers, baby home, and others. It was taboo. We had experienced something so secret, so urgent, so special, and so dangerous. Yet, in retrospect, and in consideration of the intricate challenges, I believe we would do it all again.

Change of Seasons
Dawna McCarthy Cannon

Life veered off course for me in the fall of 1990. I was thirty-two and like it or not, I would soon find my second notable life lesson was fast approaching. My mother was diagnosed with stage-four renal cancer. It was extensive and it was painful. By the following summer, nine days before her fifty-eighth birthday, my Mom's life was over, and on the day she passed there was a double rainbow. I took this to be a sign that she was now pain-free and on the other side. I was both crying and smiling at the same time.

Her passing left a massive gaping hole in my entire family. None of us had ever known anyone who had cancer, let alone it being our mother, wife and grandmother, as it was not as prevalent then as it is today. She was the hub of our wheel and losing her sent everyone into a tailspin. In order to understand what type of impact this had on me personally, you'll need to know what our relationship was like.

We were always in a constant tug of war about anything and everything. I didn't know how she felt about me as the word "love" was never mentioned until her last few days on earth. Up to that point, I'd always felt I had been nothing more than a disappointment to her. My feelings for her were very mixed up and confused, just like me at that time. I knew I loved her, but also knew I resented her for contributing to my own feelings of inadequacies. I was an overweight child who was told by her that "Omar the tent-maker" made my dresses.

Had I only known then what I know now, her last few months would have been much better. I would have known how to ease her pain and anxiety better in those last months by being there more. I don't mean physically, because I was there in that respect. But mentally all I wanted to do was run, so I drank myself into a stupor on many, many nights, which left me numb and hungover when sitting and caring for her during the daytime. That state of mind left us sitting there in silence watching the game show station on TV when we should have been talking. My mother had ALWAYS been in control and now she wasn't. She was expecting ME to be the one in control, but I had no clue how to do that. It was a painful process, to say the least.

Since her passing, I've discovered more about her childhood and why she became the person she was. It was an eye-opening experience and helped me understand why she was the way she was with me. I also came to realize another contributing factor to our angst, which was how much I was like her, much more than I had ever been willing to admit to at that time. If I'd only known then what I know now, I believe she and I would have been close friends instead of "frenemies." I LOVE you, Mom.

Remembering
Loba Chudak

"Then on each moment's flash of our thought,
There will grow a lotus flower,
And on each lotus flower will be revealed perfection,
Unceasingly manifest as our life,
Just as it is,
Right here and right now.
May we extend this mind to all beings."

Bodhisattva's Vow - Torei Enji (1721-1792)

On a dreary rain-drizzled day, I was walking down the street on the way to my Alexander Technique lesson in Hamburg, Germany, my hometown at the time. It was in this moment I noticed a thought; in fact, something that felt like a lightning strike, an insight, a vision was coming in and moving through me.

"Then on each moment's flash of our thought,"

The vision showed I was going to be in America that fall; it was early spring. Being in my final years of studying flute performance at the Musikhochschule in Hamburg, I had never really thought about, in any serious way, of leaving my hometown and country. Yes, I had traveled extensively throughout Europe, as many Europeans do, but I had not been to America.

Startled by the clarity, I felt the strength of this vision's reality and surety. This gave me impetus. I knew that it was so. And it was.

"There will grow a lotus flower,"

I organized and began to follow this path that had rolled out in front of me on that dreary day crossing the bridge, as I had done countless times, to catch the train.

Looking back I see the steps, the momentum, and the quickening of all that was needed to set this change of course in motion: the commitment on my part, the trust and willingness to act and jump off the cliff.

"And on each lotus flower will be revealed perfection,"

The details, amazing as they are, and too many to mention here, would be material for a book in and of itself. Much needed to be done and all of it was unknown, many challenges and hurdles to move through. Yet there was impetus; I just knew this was so. It already existed; this path that was putting my feet on it.

"Unceasingly manifest as our life, just as it is, right here and right now."

I came to Illinois that fall and started a three-year certification training program in the Alexander Technique. What startled me when I arrived in America, mixed in with all that was new and overwhelming, was the clear sensation of having come "home." It was odd and comforting at the same time, in a place where I didn't know anyone and had never been before. I felt I had arrived.

Since then, I have lived in the U.S. for over twenty years, and it is indeed my home. Over the years, I have come to discover that my experience on that particular day and the way I followed its momentum is most precious and significant. It has continued to serve me as a North Node. What I somehow knew and trusted then I would always like to remember. It is a teaching about guidance and being engaged in the creative process. The willingness to stop and listen, to realize what we already know, releases us into greater alignment and spaciousness. "Re-membering" the forgotten and not-yet owned aspects, we heal into our life.

How do we remember?

Times keep appearing when I simply cannot see and find myself wrestling. They are part of life, but now I have more practice under my belt. Rather than continuing to grasp for the answers, I am reminded to rest in the space between knowing and not knowing, to get out of the way and become informed by the subtle, yet powerful force that moves my personal call to action in exact and surefooted steps.

The surety and aliveness with which I was willing to follow the call I received on that dreary day is something I continue to learn from and practice. Like fine-tuning an instrument, I have become more attuned to recognizing my ways of interference with this fresh flow of life energy, be it sitting in front of a blank canvas, a blank page, or the canvas of life. Getting out of the way to freely express this moment becomes the ongoing work of practicing balance.

The vast mystery of life, a vitality that is at the source of our acting, being, and sharing, serves us with guidance, inspiration, and clarity. She, the mystery, emerges in the midst of not knowing.

I am self-employed as an artist and soul vision mentor. In living a creative life, following the path of creating takes a lot of pathfinding muscle. I continue to be encouraged by the beauty and wisdom that lie in following one's calling; in big and small ways, simple and complex, one step at a time. I see the need for following this path in the world at large.

The freedom and well-being that come from serving, informed by the vitality of life, go much beyond our own person and lift the actions we take into a broader community of supporting one another's journey with diligence, compassion, and grace. Practicing trust and working towards living by it supports an ever-growing community of people being guided by their calling to serve the greater good. This is the ripple effect of "Re-membering," becoming whole.

"May we extend this mind to all beings."

Healing by Feeling
Deborah O'Brien

Memorial Day, 1991, was the day I finally drank myself to death.

As I lay on the hospital bed waiting to die, I felt so ashamed. They force-fed me black, gritty charcoal to filter the poison from my blood, and it stuck to my teeth like cement. There was a sickeningly sweet scent of something rotting in the room. I wondered if the unpleasant odor was coming from me or if it was the smell of sin.

My uncle, Father Bill, prayed over me. Even as he was giving me the last rites, the vindictive voice in my head kept tormenting me: You loser! You could never do anything right. Look how you make your children suffer.

I couldn't listen to that voice; I had to escape. Quietly, I closed my eyes and slipped away.

For six months leading up to that fateful day, my life had been a living hell. I lived in constant fear that my youngest son wouldn't make it home alive from the Gulf War.

I chose to hole up in a dark, dingy room watching the war news on television, smoking and drinking myself into oblivion.

The smell of stale cigarette butts and cheap wine permeated the small space. Just like humidity, the stench of despair hung heavy in the air. Fear held me prisoner there; a sense of impending doom kept me company each day.

I couldn't stand to be alone with my feelings; I couldn't deal with the emotional pain. I had to break free but all I could do was remain numb.

Day after day, I drank my life away. Always blaming others and complaining, I became a source of negative energy. Soon, all that negative energy seemed to repel people from me. After a while, it was just the booze and me until the day it caught up with me and I overdosed on pills and alcohol.

Despite the valiant efforts of a team of doctors, I was dying and they said there was nothing more they could do. The Red Cross scrambled to get my son home from the war in time to say goodbye to me. When all five of my children gathered around my bed, I looked into their tear-filled eyes and I saw their love, but I also saw their sorrow and horror.

A fierce love for my children pounded in my heart. I knew I was powerless to protect them from their pain. In that moment, I knew I had to face the pain and feel my emotions in order to break free.

A miracle then happened. The vindictive voice inside my head stopped. Its words were replaced with, "Thy will be done," playing in my mind like a broken record. I heard the sound of my breath, as if someone else was breathing for me.

Listening to that soothing sound calmed me. Then, there was silence. Serenity fell over me like a warm blanket and in that stillness, I surrendered.

Suddenly, I felt a tingling in my feet and hands. A vibration throbbed in my groin. I felt a flutter in my stomach like something was swelling inside me. When the vibration moved up into my heart, I felt more alive than I ever had before. My heart was overflowing with gratitude and then it felt like something burst.

I was in the state of bliss.

God's pure, white light radiated through every inch of me; I knew the light was love and the love was God. There was no fear, only an incredible, unconditional love. There I was, surrounded by this love with all my faults and failures; God loved me anyway. I felt so special, cherished, and adored.

Peace overcame me. I did not die; I came alive. I was reborn and my life was transformed.

Six years ago, I was finishing a breathing session when I heard an audible, pronounced whisper. "TEACH." I heard the slowly-spoken word and it caused me to freeze. Once more, I heard, "TEACH MY FLOCK." The only person I ever heard of who mentioned the word "flock" was Jesus, but could He be the one speaking to me?

I didn't tell anyone about this encounter, but I didn't stop thinking about it, wondering what it meant. What did He want me to teach? One day, it hit me. I was to teach the lessons I learned about life from my encounter with death.

We often think, "If only I knew then what I know now," but for me, I know I had to go through all that I did in order to follow this calling. I spent a lifetime searching for anything to fill a void inside me and in the end I found that what I needed had always been within my reach. Fear was the only thing standing in my way.

Today, when I look back on my miracle moment in 1991, I know that was when I surrendered and let go of my fear; I began to heal.

I believe the gift of finding true bliss that day was due to my capacity to feel the pain of seeing the sorrow and horror in my children's eyes.

Here is what I discovered: All of the things I didn't want to feel lost their power the moment I decided to face them head-on. When I allowed myself to feel, I finally began to heal.

Becoming Fearless!
Maura O'Leary

It was 1996 and I was in my twelfth year of being a secretary. I was an executive assistant to a Sales VP at a growing start-up. I loved my boss and company but was burnt out from my job and couldn't make ends meet. I knew I was smart and could contribute much more, if only someone would give me that chance! I approached my VP, Dave, and proposed a barter program to solicit growing websites to join our search network. Wanting to give me a chance, he agreed.

One day I was on the phone with a prospect who had a music site, and we started talking about top upcoming concerts, etc. Unbeknownst to me, during this conversation my CEO was nearby waiting to talk to Dave, and he listened to our call. He heard how I brought the conversation back to signing up for the barter program. The prospect agreed to sign a contract. My CEO went into my VP's office and stated, "Hire her in sales."

The next day Dave said, "I have a great opportunity for you. You have a gift. Selling on the phone comes naturally to you – we want you in sales!" I was terrified, especially when I learned I'd have to take a pay cut to start! My immediate response was "I can't do that." Dave replied, "Yes you can. I believe in you. Besides, the CEO wants you to do it." I took the weekend to consider it. On Monday I said, "Ok, I'll try it."

From that day I never looked back. I LOVED sales!

The result? I was the top inside sales person my first year! Management nicknamed me "The Mojo" because of my intuitive skill to find good clients and deals. Sales completely changed my life: I went from making $30K a year to six figures. I bought my own new condo, and helped put a niece through college.

Then, in 2010 I hit a dead end. I still loved sales and my colleagues, but I didn't feel challenged. There were so many ideas I could contribute to the company. But sadly, I felt my voice wasn't being heard. So I left, and I started my own company! Did I have a solid business plan and clients lined up? No! But I knew that, based on my life experiences and how I had overcome my past fears, everything would work out. And it DID. My business grew steadily, and in six months I landed a big client. I was officially an entrepreneur running her own successful company!

And today? This past year I launched my first book. I had no major knowledge in publishing or writing of articles. I just went for it! I didn't let fear get in my way. I am still in awe my book got published. All I know is this: I wrote from the heart and never let fear consume me. I continue to live my life fearlessly and I hope this story inspires you to do the same!

If you're feeling consumed by fear, breathe deeply, and know the universe is protecting you!

Tapping Into the Power of Sisterhood
Tara McKenzie Gilvar

I was born the eldest of three children, the only girl. I had a great group of girlfriends throughout every stage of my childhood, but I never fully consciously realized my desire to have an authentic "sisterhood" experience until decades later.

In college, I had a long-term boyfriend. For seven years, I put my boyfriend first, above my college roommates. I hung out mostly with his friends, spent weekends with his family, and celebrated his career and professional successes. From age eighteen to age twenty-six, I largely tied my existence to his life's trajectory. We even got engaged.

So, imagine my devastation when just six weeks before my "Cinderella" wedding, he made the decision to call it off. It was a difficult time for me, to say the least. One that took me a very long time to recover from, especially since I had alienated myself for so many years from a safe and supportive tribe of women who could have rallied around me, helped heal my emotional wounds, and guided me to the next path on my life's journey.

I wish I could tell you that I knew from that moment what my life's purpose was, but that would not be true.

I did move on to get married to a wonderful man and have three amazing children who would make any mother enormously proud. Yet, even with this fairytale ending, my life's story was still not complete. Some part of my life still ached for fulfillment, empowerment, and sisterhood.

In 2009, after spearheading an "over the top" volunteer fundraiser for a local hospital with more than twenty other amazing women, I discovered the euphoria that can happen when like-minded, smart women come together under a common cause to make an impact in the world.

Yet, the world of volunteerism has its downside. For me, it was a "give and give and give and never get" experience. While the brainstorming, planning, and ability to bring our simple idea to life with a fabulous group of uplifting and positive women was like lightning in a bottle, the relentless and one-sided expectations of the hospital left me and many of the women I worked with feeling tremendously undervalued and taken for granted – the opposite of what we were seeking.

So, I retreated. Never again would I stick my neck out and give so freely of my time, my energy, and my money, only to have the experience be beneficial solely to the recipient. What about me? Didn't I deserve to feel truly satisfied, validated, and accomplished for the gifts and talents I brought to the world? Shouldn't my contributions to my community leave me feeling filled and enthused instead of emptied and used?

Weeks later, I saw a bumper sticker on a teacher's car that read: Remember Who You Wanted to Be. For me, it was more than a bumper sticker; it was a Divine calling. I knew I was put on this planet to be more than a mom, a wife, and daughter. I also knew through my "emotionally mixed" fundraising experience that the way to achieve my true purpose was through a sisterhood community of like-minded women.

So, through the power of just one email, sent randomly to a conglomerate of women in my community, I inadvertently started a mission designed to help women tap into their true life's purpose, unleash their inner passions and share their unique and special gifts and talents with the world. To date, our women's empowerment organization, B.I.G. (Believe Inspire Grow) has attracted more than 3,000 members and assisted numerous women in moving forward in pursuit of their life's purpose. For me, I discovered, like Dorothy in the Wizard of Oz, that by tapping into the wonderful world of "sisterhood," I had the power all along.

Loving Your Whole Self
Alina Lopez-Thomas

"Love makes your soul crawl out from its hiding place." Zora Neale Hurston

It took me many years to find love, not just any type of love, you know that kind of love which makes you want to dance, sing, get artistic. When I fell in love, the heavens opened and poured happiness tears. I stood with no cover in the middle of the arboretum between trees on the green grass, mouth open and shouted. FREEDOM! This day came only once in my life, and please don't judge. I fell in LOVE with ME. It felt like warm hot chocolate on a cold winter day: marshmallows floating to the top, with soft melodies of music.

As a child I was very quiet; one would classify me as an introvert. I was an easy child and could be taken anywhere. I rarely complained. Now, this was great for my parents and all caretakers. However, this quietness came with many inner secrets. My biological parents divorced early into their marriage, and I lived between two households. My mother was a very religious person, and at the time my father was a streetwise type of man.

I was a tall, thin, caramel-colored black-girl, with silky long black hair. I was always being told "you got good hair," words spoken out of jealousy. This was hard for me to understand, so the day my mom cut my hair I was thrilled. Maybe, I could be normal now. I hated being on display.

My parents never knew that growing up I was the victim of being bullied by other children and to what extent. Fear and insecurity were everyday emotions for me. It started in elementary school and followed me straight into high school. I never spoke up for myself, even though I was physically, verbally and emotionally abused, and more. Being Alina was challenging.

If only I knew then what I know now... that as a child, having a voice and speaking up is your right.

Protecting yourself is your ability to capture fear and regain control of your inner strength. If only I had true love then.

Bullying eventually crept back into my life, this time as an adult employee in a long-term management position I held for twenty-one years, working in a state government agency. I was a dedicated employee, extremely loyal, and way too comfortable in my position. I sacrificed my time and health, with no respect in return.

Workplace bullying taught me something: my appreciation for, and the value in building solid relationships, the importance of human compassion, and basic respect. My love for myself has increased. I recognize that we are all replaceable and taking care of your health is important, given that you never know what will happen in your life.

One door may close to eventually open another. The world has so many opportunities out there for you.

Being fearful of change stops you from reaching higher levels – your creative flow stagnates and blocks what you have to offer others who may be just like you. Don't be bullied. Use your voice and speak up. Be in LOVE, like ME.

A Girl in the Mirror – A Woman Revealed
Melissa Murphy

As we look into the mirror, the image reflecting back is our inner child, but often we only see the image created in our thinking of perceived shortcomings. Our journey reveals messages into our greatness, but often we allow limiting beliefs to be our focus, thus sabotaging our full potential. Who we "see" is who we become, and we all have the opportunity to see the essence of our truth, through our purpose and passion leading us to who we are meant to be.

I always had a relationship with the girl in the mirror, but as she grew our conversations changed. One day, or so it seemed, I woke up with low self-esteem. I could tell no one, for fear I would hurt those who loved me the most. I believed low self-esteem came from lack of love from your parents, and my parents provided us unconditional love and support, so how then did I have low self-esteem? Our paradigms are habits of our beliefs, are supported by our experiences, and are even sometimes derived through our expectations.

I was eight, Mom was ironing, and I, standing in front of the ironing board with hands on hips, said, "Mommy, I'm going to marry a man just like Daddy and have twelve children!" Mom smiled and said, "I hope you do marry a man like Daddy, and you'll be a wonderful Mommy. God's greatest gift is blessing us with children." This moment defined my expectations of my faith, and my life. Conversations in the mirror changed over time to, "why the bridesmaid, never the bride, and why am I not good enough?" I entered a career I never wanted, became successful as I climbed the ladder, gaining titles and big salary, but it all came at a high price. Over time, I put on armor to become what others said was necessary to become successful in that world, and the weight started to kill ME.

At thirty, low self-esteem nearly sabotaged the most important relationship of my life, the one with my husband. Thankfully, the twenty-four-year-old man proved to be like no other I had previously met – he was just like my Dad. On our wedding day, I looked in the mirror and thanked the girl who had the vision at eight. However, the second half of her dream, to be a mother, would be impossible; validating my fears that God did not believe I was good enough. However, these words would change everything: "If you feel your dream is impossible, simply redefine it, don't change it; see the 'more' within it." I looked into the mirror at the smiling eight-year-old and heard her whisper, "you are the mother God desired you to be, as you support His children of all ages to see their truth in the essence of their journey."

The girl in your mirror always knew you: confident, kind, beautiful, and enough – a woman with no limits, shifting her perception from lack to abundance; starting with a BIG dream, taking steps toward her journey that turns a dream into reality! Dream BIG and Go For It!

WOMEN'S STORIES OF DISCOVERY

You Are Exactly As You Are Supposed To Be
Nancy O'Keefe

How many people plan what they want to do when they grow up? Most people simply fall into their line of work, don't they? I have worked with many people over the years who were history majors who ended up with careers in insurance, liberal arts majors in quality assurance, or English majors in technical writing. The fact is that for many of us, the career we chose isn't even on our radar early in our lives. But there are some people who know what they want to be when they grow up and that was me.

I wanted to be in business before I really knew what it was. It all started one rainy day when my mother gave me a 3x5 red ink pad and a date stamp to occupy me because she had something to do. The first thing I did with it was play office. I was about seven and my favorite things to play with were papers, files, staplers, pens, pencils, and paper clips. OK, I was a weird kid, but I knew pretty early what I liked.

I also knew early on that I saw things differently than most people. We grew up in the "children were seen and not heard" era. I wanted to be seen and heard. I was always asking "why?" I just couldn't accept things at face value. My mother called me rebellious. I was. She would ask me why I couldn't do what I was told without arguing with her about it. She called me fresh. I told her I would rather be fresh than stale.

My mother said I was bossy. I was. The home movies proved it. I know she was hoping for a daughter who did what she was told and spoke when she was spoken to. That just wasn't me. In elementary school, I was always organizing the games, directing the action, persuading my friends to donate a toy they didn't want any more to a "store" we would set up on the corner; anything to earn money for the penny candy store. I convinced my friends to put on a play and charge admission or stage a fair with rides in the backyard and charge our friends to come. My mother didn't appreciate my ideas. She had to deal with the other mothers when their kids' toys or money went missing.

In junior high I practically failed algebra because I wanted to know how the equations worked. The only way I passed was that I had a teacher who recognized my "problem with authority" and held me after school one day to have a talk about my grade. I was an "A" student everywhere except his class. He told me that I needed to accept the rules of algebra, learn them, and use them to do the equations. Just do what you're told. That didn't stop me from questioning things, looking for better or easier ways, challenging the status quo.

Not much changed as an adult. I reworked all the processes in an office where I worked when we got a computer. I worked as the manager of a development group in a tech company. My department did all the data structures, screens and output forms for a computer product before the PC. One day I got a call from one of the customers. He liked our product but the screens and forms didn't work for him. He had other data needs. I asked him what he needed. He told me and I built it, cut it to a software release, and sent it to him as a patch to his system. It wasn't until a week later when I saw the CEO bombing down the hall toward my office that I realized I probably should have sent what I built through QA, documented it, and released it through normal channels before I sent it out. I thought I was going to get fired.

It turned out the customer was a personal friend of the CEO. Great. I thought I was going to pass out until the CEO said the customer raved about what I sent him. The CEO asked me only one question, "Can you do it again?" I said "Sure," and a custom data and form product was born.

I spent most of my life on a path that got me reprimanded by my parents, ridiculed by my friends, and in hot water a few times at work. It seemed like I was always flirting with trouble. I felt like I didn't fit in. But what I came to realize later in life was that my new ideas and my rebellious nature were really creativity and innovation in disguise. My persuasiveness, "directing" nature, organizational skills, and proclivity to move people to do "new things" were leadership. My desire to put on a show or sell some toys to get candy was entrepreneurship. Those qualities have served me well, taking me from receptionist to seven-figure business owner. I know I will always have new possibilities to explore and differences to make.

If you feel like you don't fit in, good. That means you are on your true path. Don't let yourself be seen and not heard or worse, not seen at all. Be you. You are exactly as you are supposed to be.

Unstoppable!
Laura Fry

In the summer of 2015 I found myself sitting in a rehabilitation facility in Tucson, Arizona, feeling utterly hopeless. Several hours earlier I had screamed at my beautiful three-year-old daughter.

How did I get there? I had been pushed to my breaking point. My "ex" had walked out on us that morning, for what felt like the tenth time, and I was devastated. It had happened so many times before that I was at a loss for what to do. My daughter was confused, and I just couldn't take any more. I was at a low point. I felt like I wanted to give up. All the fighting with my "ex" had worn me down. I couldn't take another failed relationship. The pain was too great to bear. I was done. I went to the back room and, on autopilot, I paced like a caged animal. My daughter cried out for me, but all I could do was yell back for her to stop crying. I realized then that I was not myself. I needed to leave. I felt like I wanted to be gone... for good.

At that point, I knew I needed help. I called my "ex" (multiple times) begging for help. I knew I needed to check myself in somewhere; otherwise, I was afraid of what I might do. I was hopeless; I had never felt this way before. After putting my daughter down for a nap, I called Sierra Tucson, a rehab facility that specializes in major depression. They did an intake over the phone, told me to pack my bags, and get a ride over there. (I was in no condition to drive.) My "ex" finally returned and agreed to take me to the facility.

During the drive down to Tucson and during intake I remember thinking, "This can't be my life. I cannot possibly be going through this. I am a successful business woman. How did I get here?"

I ended up spending five weeks at Sierra Tucson, learning about my depression, as well as the trauma I had experienced throughout my life. While it was the hardest thing to be away from my daughter for that amount of time, it was the greatest gift to be able to process what had been holding me back all these years. I learned about the trauma I experienced as a child: the physical, emotional, and sexual abuse that had compounded and finally came out when my "ex" left. I had hit my "bottom" that day.

While I know I felt hopeless, what I was experiencing was a trauma response, and I would never truly want to leave my daughter. I'm glad I didn't give up. After going through this I now feel unstoppable and know that I can go through anything. So, to this day, "Unstoppable!" is my motto. I have also made that my personalized license plate.

There may be times in life when you feel you can't take any more, when you have been pushed to the limit. Please do not give up... there is hope around the corner. YOU are "Unstoppable!"

The Visualization
Nancy K. Armstrong

As I quietly sat with my eyes shut, I attempted to empty my mind of any thought or care in the world. Breathe in, breathe out. Ah! I took a deep breath, held it, and blew it out hard. I imagined every speck of negativity leaving my body, replacing the emptiness with beautiful white light. Shining down from above, it entered through my head and filled every part of my being. It was warm and comforting. Breathe in, breathe out. I slowed my breath – it was so calming and mesmerizing.

Halfway between sleep and wakefulness, I found myself in visualization where I was walking along a cobblestone path. There were trees on both sides and lots of flowers! They were so beautiful I could almost smell them. I took a deep breath and released it. Oh, how I loved the flowers and sweet memories they brought me.

The birds sang joyfully as they fluttered through the treetops – their songs beautifully choreographed with the rustling wind and animals scurrying through the forest. As I continued down the path, it opened into a big, beautiful prairie with "golden" green grass swaying in the wind. In the distance there was a tree on a hill. As I got closer, I saw a bench under the tree. This looks delightful, I thought, as I sat down and nestled into the bench quite comfortably. I took a long, deep breath and gazed down at the bubbling brook below.

From the corner of my eye I saw a little girl walking towards me. She wore a long white gown and had beautiful blonde hair. Her piercing blue eyes glistened with a hint of sadness. She wasn't very old and was way too young to be alone. I looked around, wondering who was watching over her.

In a sweet little voice, she said, "Will you help me?" Stunned, I asked, "Where are your parents?" "My mommy didn't want to be a mommy!" she said as tears welled up in her eyes. "She left me when I was a baby. She came back once, but she left me hungry and alone. She didn't want to be my mommy anymore. She tried to kill herself; there was so much blood!" She sobbed. "Oh, honey!" I gasped, "You poor girl!" She put her tiny hands in mine; they were soft and innocent. She told me, "I'm scared! My new family is mean to me." She was shaking. "It hurts when they hit me and touch me down there. I don't want to do those things they make me do. But my daddy can't hear me cry and nobody will make them stop!" She was sobbing harder now.

"Oh, no!" I grabbed her and hugged her tight, both of us crying. I looked in her eyes – my eyes – and said, "I know it hurts and I know you're scared. I want to say it is over, but I know it is not. You still have many difficult roads ahead. Those images are forever ingrained in your brain, but you will survive! We survived! And all those people that hurt you are gone! You are safe! We are safe! I've healed the scars the best I can. I am happy, I am loved, and I am safe! I am also a mommy. We love and protect our beautiful boy with everything we have! Our life is wonderful!

We have overcome so many challenges. Now people say I am an inspiration!" She smiled at me and said, "I love you!" We hugged as our hearts merged into one, healing us together.

Sitting on the bench, engulfed in my own thoughts, I saw an old woman walking up the hill. She wore a flowing white gown and had long silver hair. She was tall, thin, and majestic as she came to me. When I looked into her eyes, they were joyful and loving. She was a beautiful, wise, and powerful goddess.

"Hello, my dear, it's good to see you again," she said. I knew who she was – I could see the wisdom, love, and understanding in her eyes – my eyes. She embraced me tightly until tears flowed from my eyes. I cried – this time tears of joy. She said, "I know it has been a long, hard journey, I am so proud of you for healing your heart and living a life worth living. You are a wonderful mother! Raising your beautiful little boy on your own has been challenging. You have grown and learned tremendously from this experience. He has been your most brilliant teacher and most willing student. He has brought love into your life like you have never known. You taught him to be healthy, loving, and wise, giving him everything that you never had: love, compassion, and respect. He is proud of you. You inspire people by just being you and standing in your truth. You have overcome many obstacles and will overcome many more to become the goddess you are meant to be. Stand tall and stay strong! You will do great things." With that, we hugged and once again our hearts merged together in healing love.

I awoke filled with peace, love, and compassion, and an undeniable sense of being exactly as I was meant to be – perfectly unique in every way!

From Dork to Cool
Melissa Bloodgood

It started at age fifteen: my first kiss... prom as a sophomore... the first hit of weed and that drunken feeling that comes from your first three slugs of vodka... sex... all in that same year.

Almost twenty-nine now, I am for the first time since then completely sober. Five months without weed and alcohol. Sex is not so much of a drug if you're in love and respected by your partner. That was not the case for so many years, and I drank knowing it was the route to getting laid. It would "just happen," and I craved that validation. It meant I was attractive and well-liked, didn't it?

Some studies say that when a girl's first sexual experience is rape she tends to become extremely promiscuous. This was my experience. I laughed it off for so long. "No! Stop!" screamed at the top of my lungs still drilled in my memory. Drunk, but the memories of the night are clear. After that came blackouts, multiple partners, poor hygiene, baggy clothes, all the stuff you come to realize is "by the book": Lifetime channel movie stuff. I wish I knew then that I could have spoken up.

As a little girl, outside of my house I'd whisper to my big sister and she was my voice. She was four years older and everything I wanted and tried to be. I drank how I imagined she drank when I was reading her diary. Alcohol gave me a new voice. I really believed it was the ingredient that brought me from dork to cool.

I never made my own decisions, stripped of self-esteem and confidence like so many addicts. I manipulated most moments, driven by the need to get high and drunk and escape that which I was so desperately trying to be a part of. What if someone had informed me back then that when I was sober I was better than anything alcohol had to offer? However, had I known, there would be no stories to share with other struggling alcoholics. Legalizing weed doesn't make it okay. Tobacco kills. Weed stupefies. "Alcohol... oh, alcohol." Some of us just can't drink like the rest of you. Long live the government. I want to make art and listen to old music and drink tea and keep up with the times, to grow up and become like the sixty- and seventy-nine-year-old ladies in Zumba class at the gym.

It's still hard to accept myself. I think, "I'm all right, but I'll be a lot cooler in ten, twenty years." At sixty-five I will have arrived. Oh, but will times have changed?

Art Therapy Works
Lisa Sullivan Bond

Groggily, I awoke in an area similar to a living room, lying on a couch. Two women sat nearby. I slowly lifted myself into a sitting position and asked, "What day is it?" In unison they answered, "Sunday." "Where am I?" One of them matter-of-factly replied, "In a hospital." Then it came back to me: I had been admitted late Friday afternoon after taking a few sleeping pills. I remember asking the emergency room doctor, "How many pills would be considered an overdose?" His sobering reply was, "Any number more than the prescribed amount." I had slept for thirty-three hours straight. What brought me here?

It was Friday morning. On the return ride to our summer home from a shopping excursion with both my two- and four-year-olds firmly strapped in their car seats, I approached a stretch of road, a causeway, with water on both sides, where, at one point, if you don't turn sharply to the right, you drive straight into the water. Suddenly I had a strong, compelling urge to do just that. Fighting the urge, I turned right. What I had just experienced scared me to death – well, almost.

Feeling panicked when I got to our summer home, I called the psychiatrist who had recently started me on a very strong antidepressant. He asked, "Do you think you will be able to drive back to Boston and come into my office this afternoon with your husband?" In the joint session, I described how overwhelmed I was feeling as an older mom taking care of two small children, essentially by myself. It had been a major change from working full-time and living in Cambridge to moving to the suburbs and getting pregnant.

During the session, my husband agreed that we'd hire an au pair. On the drive home, he said: "That's not going to happen." Back at the house, feeling even more despondent, I retreated to the bathroom with my container of sleeping pills. They were in my hand when my husband came looking for me. Instead of taking the pills out of my hand, he ran off to call the psychiatrist and I thought to myself, "Well, I guess I'm going to have to take a few," and I did.

On Monday morning I was assigned to an arts and crafts class. "This is absurd," I thought. "They are treating us like little kids." Truth be told, I had always loved art and being creative, but had been steered toward taking academic courses in high school in order to get into an Ivy League college.

Of the projects, I chose a small, rough block in the shape of a car, not unlike my first car, a VW Bug. I had to sand the wood before I could glue the wheels onto the dowels; then I would be able to paint it. I was surprised by the pleasure and satisfaction I got from sanding. The next day I painted the wheels blue and the car bright red with a yellow racing stripe. The final day was spent shellacking the car to protect the paint. Meanwhile, some of the other residents had completed two or three projects.

Through the effective combination of art and talk therapies, I recognized I had learned two important things: how much pleasure I'd gotten from working with my hands and how my husband's criticism and verbal abuse had undermined my self-confidence. I had learned that suppressing anger and resentment could lead to depression. I learned it was important to stand up for myself and not be bullied into submission. After all, I wanted to provide a strong role model for my daughter.

When it came time at the end of the week to say goodbye in the morning meeting, I brought my car as a visual prop to describe the analogy of how creating it had taught me about myself. I had learned to take pride in the way I did things – with attention to detail and thoughtfulness. It might take me longer to complete something, but I was proud of what I'd made. Instead of my pattern of always putting others' needs first, I learned it is not selfish to allow myself time to be creative; that rest, exercise and playfulness are needed in my life as a break from constant care-taking. It was OK to take time for myself, to be me. Art therapy works!

This ending sounds too simplistic. It took further therapeutic work to come to an understanding of my depression. For years I blamed myself for having thought of committing suicide. An important fact I wish I had known from the start is that taking an antidepressant may cause suicidal thoughts; this did not become public knowledge until 2003. Also worth noting is that one may think of suicide before taking an antidepressant, but after taking it, you may become energized and could actually succeed!

Clinical depression has a terrible irony: When you most need help from your family and friends, you are unable to ask for it. My advice to everyone is: If you notice someone is withdrawing from contact, spend time with him or her; listen and say, "Tell me more." A great resource for helpful information is the National Association for Mental Health, a nonprofit organization created by families to help families.

What Was I Thinking?!
Sheila Pearl

"Money isn't important" was something I heard growing up. If you hear your parents say it, if you hear the minister or rabbi say it, if you hear your friends say it over and over again, you might just believe it.

When I was seven, my mother asked me "What do you want to be when you grow up?" I knew: I wanted to be a singer and a mom. That was my focus. I became a singer. I became a mom (a stepmother and soul mother).

"Live your dream!" everyone said, so I did. I married the love of my life, pursued a career as an opera singer and cantor, and helped my husband raise his teenagers. I now have five grandchildren. Along the way, there were many bumps in the road during my

105

thirty-two-year marriage. "Money isn't important" insidiously ruled my subconscious in ways yet to emerge. The big lie of that statement would hit me between the eyes.

After over twenty-five years of marriage, raising teenagers, thriving in our careers and our loving relationships, my husband began to show signs of an ugly illness neither of us wanted to face. As his symptoms intensified, we could not continue to deny the truth: My beloved husband was suffering from a form of dementia called "Diffuse Lewy Body Disorder" – a cousin of Alzheimer's.

Two years before my husband was officially diagnosed, a good friend who was an insurance broker invited me to her office with my checkbook. She advised me to purchase both Long Term Care Insurance and Life Insurance for my husband and myself. Immediately. She understood what I had not been seeing: Money *was* important! The premiums were larger for my husband, who was sixteen years my senior; yet, I knew the investment was hugely important. As long as my husband had his job and I maintained mine, I could afford to pay the premiums. However, once my husband could no longer work, I struggled with the expenses and had to make painful decisions about what to keep.

"Money isn't important" kept ringing in my ears. I found myself facing an important decision: Which policies could I afford to keep? More overwhelmed than I realized, focusing more on my husband's needs than mine, I was feeling invincible, deluding myself into believing that I needed to protect my husband by making the selfless choice of continuing the life insurance policy on *myself* and canceling the life insurance policy on *him*. Big mistake!

What in the world was I thinking?! It was inevitable that I would outlive him – I was not only sixteen years younger than he, but healthy. What was I thinking as I canceled *his* life insurance policy, which would have assured *me* of some financial protection once he passed?

Our shared financial blindness and shortsightedness continued to snowball: I kept the long-term-care policy on my husband, canceling my own. Luckily for us, since I had that policy, I was able to keep my husband home with me until his death. That was a blessing for him and for me, despite the difficulties of navigating the ensuing five-year period, both emotionally and financially.

Neither my husband nor I had been financially intelligent: We were smart focusing on following our dreams and doing the work that gave us satisfaction and a sense of making a difference; yet were exceedingly "stupid" about facing the importance of financial planning for our later years. Neither of us was in the habit of saving money, and we both often spent more than we made. For two people who were highly educated professionals and spiritual leaders, we were financially *stupid*!

Now, in my mid-seventies, and a widow for over a dozen years, I am blessed to be doing work which I deeply enjoy. Yet, I am cursed by the results of my choices: I have no savings, no investments, and no nest egg on which to rely.

I confess to having mixed emotions: I often wrestle with feeling betrayed and abandoned by a husband who was older and (I thought) wiser, who didn't financially provide for me. Then I shout to myself: *"Be a grown-up!"* I do take full responsibility for my choices.

As a "grown-up" and coach, I seek to walk my talk. I also abhor the idea of being a "victim" in any way whatsoever; I am willing to own my financial illiteracy and tell this story often as an example of ways we each suffer from blindness of one kind or another.

When coaching clients who come to me with life situations that are difficult and challenging, I pose this question: "What blessings or gifts can you see coming out of this difficult situation?"

For me, at a stage of life in which many seniors are more relaxed about financial matters, I am constantly on the edge, seeking ways to be of service to others, to generate more creativity, and to remain exceedingly healthy. For me, it's a matter of practicality: I'm highly motivated to be healthy and functional. If I can't do my work and generate an income from what

I love to do, I am totally dependent upon my Social Security check.

That just doesn't cut it, folks!

Her
Katrina Piehler

I could feel Her standing behind me. I heard him say I don't want to be married to you anymore, and I felt Her slip quietly behind, wrapping herself like a cloak, around my back.

It was twenty-two years ago and I still recall the sensation. It was as if she merged with me; fortified me. She had my back. And in that moment I didn't feel like my twenty-eight-year-young self who just had the rug pulled out from under her.

In that moment I had access to something (someone?) that helped me viscerally know everything was going to be OK. And it was.

When I reflect back on that experience, I remember how I used to think of Her as an angel who came to envelop me in empowering wings of wisdom and confidence just when I needed it. I was so grateful. As time went on, that sensation stayed with me, but it shifted. I began to see the wings that appeared, not as someone else's, but as my own.

Years later, a life coach I worked with guided me in a visualization exercise that invited me to connect with how I imagined my future self. The idea was that this future version of me could serve as my own inner mentor. As I let go and sank into the vision, I found myself pleasantly surprised to be feeling that same "got your back" sensation that had washed over me those many years before.

It was Her. There she was again. And she was me. Inner mentor, future self, angel... now I could feel it; they were all the essence of my spirit, the core of me.

When I was invited to contribute a story to the theme of this book, *"If Only I Knew Then What I Know Now,"* even more clarity came for me when I thought about this. I realized I don't need to feel disappointment or regret for not having been wiser in my youth.

Future, past, present; they're all connected.

It turns out I <u>did</u> know then what I know now. Or at least I had access to it. And so too, what the essence of me knows about my future is available to me in *this* present moment.

The next time I find myself feeling scared, small or uncertain – I am going to tap into that sensation of standing behind myself, of reaching for that cloak of wisdom and those wings of self-confidence.

I've got my back. And I am going to be OK.

Failing My Instinct
Heather McCarthy

In my young rebellious years, my father's instinct often recognized my guilt; other times it directed me towards the right decisions. I never doubted my father, but as any daughter would, I constantly fought against him. "Your father's instinct is good," my mother would say. Now, years later, believing one's instinct to be a gift not to be wasted or ignored, I find myself turning to both my parents to help me choose the best path forward after a devastating, life-changing event.

When I was in college, a high school sweetheart lost his mother. While I had every intention of driving the eight hours home to show support, something felt off. I called my father knowing he would talk me out of the drive. Without prompting, he did. Hours later there was a pileup on the highway at the exact place I should have been at that point in my ride. It is possible I would have missed it, but I believe heeding to our combined instincts kept me safe.

When moving into my first city apartment, my roommate and I spent days repainting the space. One night we were invited to another apartment for a late-night drink. Carrying only phones and keys, we walked down unknown streets to a beautiful South End roof deck. After hours of laughs and drinks, I needed to "call it a night" and begged my friend to leave. But, after thirty minutes of "in five minutes," I left alone.

Within moments instinct broke through intoxication to sober me up. I was being followed. Jumping off the sidewalk, I made a U-turn and darted back to the busy street I had just crossed, knowing it was closer than the one ahead of me. I stood under street lights, the late-night taxi rush between myself and the man who had performed an identical U-turn seconds behind me. No cab fare, nowhere to go and little concept of neighborhoods to my right or left, I was stuck. After initially disbelieving my pleading phone calls, my roommate finally rescued me, horrified to realize I hadn't exaggerated about the man: yards from me, hand down his pants, waiting for my next move. It was then I learned the power of my instinct.

Clear yet cloudy: igniting caution within, instinct lays out no direct path. Somehow, you know what to do while others may question your motivation. Lacking evidence, it can simply be viewed as craziness, worry, or coincidence.

Is it crazy that I spent the night before someone close to me died, sobbing myself to sleep for no apparent reason, only to wake to a tragic accident unfolding before my eyes? Was it coincidence I felt an overwhelming need to rush to meet my brother-in-law and nieces at the marathon finish line when, after spotting them but before hugging them: two explosions? Had my husband and I not arrived at that exact moment, due to my sense of urgency, what would have happened to my two nieces whom we grabbed as chaos ensued?

One year ago, a revelation left me feeling my instinct had failed me completely. I felt more betrayed by my instinct than anything else. I spent twelve months questioning it, cursing it, blaming it, and hating it. Only through confronting it did I realize it never abandoned me; I abandoned it.

My heart and soul had welcomed someone, someone I had a true and honest connection with for most of our time together. He initially valued my instinct, he trusted it, but over time my instinct became an unwelcome part of our relationship. What was once something he admired he now questioned because it was solely focused on protecting me. To him, my instinct became an irrational side of me: I was being "crazy" – and he often made me feel ridiculous. Ultimately, I blame myself for allowing someone to convince me my instinct was wrong.

If you welcome someone into your life who does not respect your instinct, whether from the start or over time, they will make you question it, distract you from it, and leave you seeing it as a flaw, inevitably causing you to ignore it. If your instinct is not convenient for all parties involved, it will be disregarded. If your gut is telling you something about someone is "off," your instinct will no longer be valuable to that person; it will become their opponent. When your instinct is going against that opponent, you will be told just how "off" your instinct is, when in fact it is as sharp as it has ever been. That is when the battle starts, not only with that opposing force, but within you.

Just a few days ago, alarm bells rang in my head regarding my daughter. I knew I needed to trust my instinct. No one was going to stop me from protecting the most important person to me, no one was going to interfere with this instinct that I had ignored for years, and no one was going to belittle this gift inside me. Within hours, my instinct was confirmed. My instinct was so unbelievably on target, I wanted to shout it from the rooftops. Just like that, this giant fog dissolved around me, and my mind and soul were at peace with each other once again.

Never Be Afraid To Go For It!
Michelle Medeiros

I was very unhappy in my chosen profession in the financial services industry. I had worked in the greater Boston area for twelve years at a high-profile company, but with that came many compromises. I had a long commute, worked long hours, and didn't spend as much time with my three boys as I wanted.

When I married my second husband, I took the opportunity to be a stay-at-home mom, which is what I thought I had always wanted. However, I got bored after six months, and realized I needed to at least work part-time to make myself feel like a normal adult. I found a job, yet again in the financial services industry, at a local company closer to home. The work environment was essentially the same: "work comes first, family second." I worked towards my MBA thinking it would open up more doors for me with a better career, but the only doors it opened were back in the greater Boston area, where I knew I didn't want to go again. Feeling I was wasting my talents in my current position, I asked myself, "What do I do now?"

A dear friend told me, "Open up a quilt store. The local one just closed and there isn't one for miles around." What, me a business owner? Yes, I had learned to quilt in high school and had taken it up again as a hobby. It was fun, and I met a lot of nice people at local classes. The environment was always positive. But open a small business in this economy? My friend pushed me and never stopped talking about it, eventually convincing me that my business background and education would help to guide me down the right road. I knew how to navigate the loan process, so I wouldn't adversely affect my personal assets, and I did it. I took the leap. Not only did I take the leap, I have never once regretted it.

Oh sure, it was very difficult at first, working by myself to get a store up and running. I had a little help here and there, but when it's your own, all the responsibility falls on you. It wasn't an immediate success when I first opened. I've had to build my business, one hard-earned customer at a time, and I'm still working hard at it and growing. I've worked diligently at overcoming my anxiety towards meeting new people. After all, I still meet new people all the time, and now it's my favorite part about the job!

Never be afraid to do something because you think you cannot! Figure out what you want, and come up with a solid plan. You will never know unless you try.

You Had the Power All Along, My Dear!
Tina Sarcia-Maxwell

If only I knew then that self-discovery happens even when I am not looking for it or feel ready to move forward. Change constantly creates my uniqueness. I know now that this is MY life and no one else's to live.

I reasoned, after years of breaking through personal barriers, that we are all UNIQUE individuals who should be CELEBRATED. I am a snowflake like no other; "no two snowflakes are alike" resonates within me. It took me a long time to feel I am whole, to feel I am beautiful. Being compliant with the world due to fear slowed and destroyed the joy on my journey. FEAR is nothing more than False Evidence Appearing Real. I played small after years of feeling like I couldn't be me. Playing it safe dulled the stars in my constellation.

Years of being made "fun of" and tackled by siblings lowered my self-esteem, but it made me a fighter. Playing sports around age eight lit me up inside. I felt exhilarated when I had a great catch or ran across the finish line. However, at times I felt I wasn't supposed to like what I liked. I was the only girl on the team. Others thought I should be someone who played with dolls. I heard comments such as "she's just one of the guys" and was called a "tom boy." This fear-based thinking conditioned me to be who others wanted me to be.

All of this had a negative effect on me. I had shame and didn't let it show because of the culture I inhabited. I was a product of my environment. *Why couldn't I be myself? Why did I make sure others felt good? Why did I empower them, but not myself? Did I exist? Why did I feel invisible? What was going on here?*

I was not happy. Letting my parents down, or anyone else for that matter, was not being true to me. Stressing out to be who others expected me to be, and trying so hard to do the "right thing" according to society, led me to perceive a one-way sign through life.

In my thirties something happened. I woke up and realized there are many ways to live and think. Having mental strength is one of them. *You mean to tell me, I don't have to like what everyone else likes? I can be me?* I gave myself permission to change. Change is exciting. Change is what I was searching for. I changed my outlook. I changed my hairstyle. I was looking for reinvention. This was fun. I felt fresh and alive. Finding what worked for ME was an ever-changing journey.

In my past struggles, had I only known I was a spiritual being having physical experiences, I would have trusted the process of life. I always felt lost and sought something or someone to look up to or follow, be it through religion, yoga, or following the path of spiritual leaders.

Inevitably, people fell short, either directly or indirectly, and there never seemed to be a safe place to turn. Disappointment kept following me. I had to find my way. Few in my circle wanted to talk about life or emotions. I did not know I had the answers and the power to carry them out the whole time. It was all within me, and I just had to learn it for myself. I could now hear my heart's desires.

I decided to listen to the fire within me and came to believe I am worthy of finding what makes me happy. Today life experiences lead me to find my path, to discover what I like and do not like. This new life can be uncomfortable, but yet, it feels right. Life is challenging, and self-forgiveness is a gift I have given myself.

The anger lessens. My fulfillment grows. I experience ease. I do not look outside of myself for validation. It all comes from within. My world is new. Being me and being *present* in the moment is the best *present* I can give myself and give those around me. From my experience comes knowledge and strength. Today I tell myself, "No matter what, be true to myself and trust the process of life. Everything always works out!" This is self-love.

The key to self-fulfillment is to engage. Being active, conversing with others, and focusing on that happiness is being loyal to my own peace of mind. In my calmness I make sound decisions and am true to myself. I did not know it then, but today I know I am on an ever-changing journey, and I am a UNIQUE individual who is CELEBRATED!

A Message for My Daughters
Lena Winston

One day, while in my thirties, I sat in a circle of like-minded people that I had invited to my home. The designated leader, a woman with a gentle voice, started the group with a prayer. Sitting in this quiet circle, the voices in my head were loud. "I'm comfortable; hmmm, do you think it's too cold in here?" "I can turn up the heat." "That lady is wearing a sweater." "Should I ask?" "I wonder if anyone wants a snack." "Oh, I'm not listening to the prayer." When the prayer ended, I stood and went to adjust the blinds to make the light dimmer. "It's nicer for everyone with the room like this."

As I look back and observe myself in those eight minutes, I realize I was conditioned and preoccupied with thoughts of responsibility for others' happiness and comfort.

I wish I knew then what I know now: I can take responsibility for myself and allow others to take care of themselves. Being someone who can see gaps and is sensitive to the environment, and as someone who has been physically capable in the past, taking care of others has always been natural for me; but at what cost, and why?

I tell my daughters to focus on themselves and be responsible for their own actions, their health, and their well-being. Then there is always the lesson of being kind to others; showing compassion and care. Love.

Saying "yes" when I can, I also say "no" when I need to: following my heart in the knowledge that within me is my truth and connection to God. When I lose sight of myself and do not speak my truth, I lose myself, short-changing my happiness in order to please others. Having passion and being in service is important. But, it is also crucial for well-being to listen within, speak my truth, ask questions, and speak up even when uncomfortable.

When I relate to others from this place of truth, I am fully myself and I experience peace. This is my lesson for stress-free living. My awareness of thinking of others above myself came to light that day, in the group.

But three years ago, when my cancer of eight years became Stage IV lung cancer – the lesson became critically important. There is nothing more important than listening to God's guidance within myself, following my truth, and living a stress-free lifestyle.

I realize now that being present to others, sitting in circle, sitting in prayer, and focusing on within is mine to do. Nothing else matters. Everyone will take care of themselves, and ask for what they want. I do not have to be the one to help. It is a lesson I am grateful to learn now, at age forty-eight. But I would have liked to have known that back at the prayer circle while in my thirties. Taking care of me is the greatest gift I can give myself and others in my life.

Silence, Order and Chaos
Katharine Gilpin

It was nighttime, maybe around nine or ten PM; I really do not remember. I do remember standing on the second floor stairwell landing. I could hear my parents' screaming match downstairs in the kitchen – I heard the shattering of china. When the coast was safely clear, after they each had walked away from the "fight arena," I quietly eased myself down the stairs to take stock of the situation.

Frozen in mind and auto-pilot in action, I numbly picked through the sea of broken shards – formerly dishware – which littered the entire kitchen floor. Sweeping the debris and tidying the fallout, I hoped my actions would make a difference. But, inevitably they didn't. Well, in retrospect, they did; they made me feel empowered by making order of the chaos, by remaining silent, and dutiful. If I just picked up the pieces and kept quiet so as not to make any waves – maybe, just maybe – I could make the situation better, make our home more peaceful. That was a big job for a young girl.

The youngest of three, the first and only daughter, I was "Mother's Little Helper." But I played second fiddle to her ever-growing dependence on prescription drugs and subsequently alcohol throughout the 1960s and 1970s. I played the role of dutiful daughter who silently observed my parents' struggles and tried to keep out of the way until the dust had safely settled.

My parents, although they did indeed love one another, had a tumultuous relationship, which was aggravated by my father's on-again, off-again well-paid positions as corporate executive, which left our family financially unstable. He was of the generation, born in 1914, of men who considered it a failure if their wife worked; this was exacerbated in his case by his staunch German heritage: his exacting manner.

My mother was a frustrated housewife, tending to a house too big for her to manage alone while raising her three children. I believe my mother, who was born in 1925 – smack in the middle of the Great Depression – grew up in the expectation of being a victim to circumstance. She simply made-due until she couldn't anymore, which sent her into eruptions and tailspins of depression.

She would "check-out," spending afternoons on the sofa in the den. Back then the medical remedy was to take sedatives. Who knows when she started adding alcohol to the mix? With reoccurring bouts of "nervous breakdowns," she would end up being admitted to the hospital or to a rehabilitation facility, for days or weeks.

Yes, that was my "fun" childhood. That was my calling to remain silent in the shadows, to try to hold things together while wishing for the best. I wish I had understood that keeping silent and accepting the leftover broken pieces was not the answer.

The full-blown realization of how reserved I had been living confronted me head-on when a tragedy struck a friend of mine. Kathy was thirty-one, a graphic designer preparing to enter graduate school for a

Master's degree in education – her wish was to teach art to young children. Around three AM on a Sunday morning in August, an intruder broke in to her basement apartment. He stabbed her over, and over, and over, and over again. Fighting to live, she managed to dial the telephone for help. Her voice was weakened to the extent that the dispatcher on duty could not make out what she said and hung up on her, thinking it a prank call. My friend died that dark morning.

For me, the devastating fact that her voice was not heard and that she was literally hung up on sent me into a reckoning. My life needed to open up. I needed to speak up and out. I needed not to play second fiddle in my own life. My wish was to break the cycle. Silence was not golden.

It has been an ongoing journey to heal my tendency to silently wait in the shadows for the "best time" to emerge and make order of the chaos. Is it ironic or is it destiny that I was drawn to and trained in sound healing: teaching and facilitating others to express their needs and wants of body, mind and spirit? We do teach what we need to learn and what we strive to overcome – to become who we want to be. I deserve to be heard, and I no longer wish to settle for picking up the broken leftovers in silent acquiescence.

Taking a bold leap into action to co-create this book – to create and hold the space for women to express themselves and get "out there" to be heard – to make a difference is a no longer merely a wish of mine.

Power Tipper
Wendy Tayer

As a faculty member in the psychiatry department of a large public university, my curiosity was piqued, so I participated in a dissertation research project exploring the developmental histories of psychologists. *It dawned on me in the most unsuspecting way; the dissertation student and I happened upon it during a phone research interview.*

For years people have asked me why I chose this profession. I responded with a chronology of my early work history characterized by disillusionment with advertising and marketing research. In addition, being the daughter of a well-known cardiologist, healthcare was a natural path for me. But I had never consciously considered the way in which my childhood experiences informed my career.

When I was eight, my parents divorced. When I was nine, my mother remarried, and moved me and my two younger brothers from Boston to New York. Finding ourselves in an unfamiliar neighborhood, sharing a house with two stepbrothers and a stepfather, we had to adjust to a new school far away from our friends and relatives, a challenge for which we were unprepared. The following three years were the most difficult ones of my life, as I was mercilessly bullied by the neighborhood girls and taunted by my brothers and their friends.

People who know me as an adult hear this tale and say, "You were picked on? I can't imagine it. Why?" I was the new kid on the block adjusting to a new life and was one of the only Jewish girls around. The girls in my neighborhood keenly sensed my vulnerability. They badgered me on the school bus, sabotaged my birthday parties, beat me up, and ridiculed me incessantly. My deeply empathic mother faithfully supported me; my brothers did not or could not defend their "Big Sis." For companionship I had two friends and a dog. In those days schools did not address bullying; I was left to fend for myself in my social arena.

It is only now I realize, as I reflect on my suffering, how transformative those painful experiences were for me. I learned about the nature of power, its glory, rewards, abuses, and costs. I learned how to pick on other vulnerable girls, actions which I deeply regret. In years to come, I would be relieved for my ability to apologize for past incidents, some of which I had conveniently forgotten until being reminded.

When I was in my twenties, I ran into the ringleader of the "girl group" that bullied me. She approached me, saying, "I was really mean to you when we were kids." At least she took responsibility, but I was in no mood to absolve her. I responded, "You're right, you were." My attitude was: let her sit with it and figure out how to live with herself. Not being up to it at the time, I chose not to be part of her healing process or offer forgiveness. Things might be different if I were to encounter her today, thirty years later. Ha! "If I only knew then what I know now!"

I know now that such experiences play a role in shaping your identity, in how you live life, derive meaning, and develop your values. Unbeknownst to me, this subconscious process had occurred by the time in my life when I had reached a choice point in terms of career.

I survived the bullying years, developing a thicker skin and enjoying the second half of high school and college. When I (along with my current husband) moved to San Diego, I felt alienated and bored in this seemingly unsophisticated city where I had a job in a "small potatoes" agency (as compared to my posh NYC firm). After meeting a local psychology graduate student, I took pause to capitalize on the realization that life sometimes provides the opportunity to redirect oneself, and subsequently applied to and attended graduate school in search of my passion.

During the seven-year period I was immersed in Clinical Health Psychology, I married, birthed two children, and moved cross country twice, a greatly empowering experience. I never anticipated that my childhood experiences would provide me with the empathy to work with disenfranchised people, but something propelled me on.

Twenty-plus years after I finished my degree, I continue to treat patients with chronic illness, pain, anxiety, clinical depression, and aging issues, never ceasing to be rewarded or surprised by my work. In my supervision of graduate students I synthesize my experiences, share how I became inspired, and pass on professional wisdom.

One day while sitting in my office after a phone interview with a graduate student, the dots connected. The paradigm that today aptly resonates with both my patients and trainees came into focus... *people enter psychotherapy feeling disempowered in some way – it is my job to help them empower themselves in whatever way is relevant for them.*

This inherent imbalance in the therapeutic relationship can be a "power trip" for some psychologists. I prefer to see myself as a purveyor of "power tips" as I help my patients to rebuild their lives, providing satisfaction, a sense of purpose, and inner peace. I recall being bullied and being the bully, thinking that if I ran into that girl who bullied me today, I would view her differently, and perhaps credit her with giving me an opportunity to develop and grow into the successful, fulfilled professional I am now.

I Was the One
Lauren Lemieux

I remember feeling alone. Invisible. Insignificant. I look back on my high school years and see merely a shell of the girl. Me, the girl who was always concerned about what someone thought of me and how they saw me: fat, ugly, smart, funny, conceited.

I did not present as insecure or vulnerable, but I was. I felt like an outsider, yet I was social, and involved in sports and activities. I was skeptical of my friends, not believing they truly cared about me. How could they? Thoughts that I was just being used or made fun of behind my back, consumed my mind daily, along with the heavy fear that my secret belief of not belonging would be exposed.

I lived with that skepticism for years, through college and even a few years after. I look back to those days and still can feel the heaviness of believing I was

147

being judged, always worried I was not good enough, popular enough, or pretty enough. I was not aware of personal empowerment. I don't remember hearing, "It doesn't matter what others think." In retrospect, had I heard it, I'm not sure I would have had the strength and confidence to believe it anyway.

What I am keenly aware of now is that it was not about what others thought of me – I realize now it was about me, about how I saw myself. I did not believe in myself. At. All. I was the one judging myself, physically, emotionally, and mentally. From my "thunder thighs" to the bump on the bridge of my nose, I never felt I was attractive, always picking out my imperfections. In relationships, I over-compensated, going above and beyond, putting everyone else's opinions and desires before my own. I lacked self-worth. I did not like myself. Regardless of if I truly was being judged, those judgments paled in comparison to what I was doing to myself. I was the one making it a big deal.

If I only knew then just how magically unique and uniquely magical I was.

My compassion and kindness are among the reasons people trust and love me. And, those "thunder thighs" of mine are a gift, a gift of power and strength that allows me to stand strong and tall with confidence and pride for the woman I continue to become.

Laureen's Spiritual Boot Camp
Deborah Corrigan

Laureen was my friend and business partner, best described by her husband as a blonde haired, blue-eyed, modern-day medicine woman. She was a warrior with a heart of gold.

We shared common ground with our love for anything vintage, laughter, and a respect for tradition. We met in a consignment shop – the two of us standing at opposite ends of a glass display cabinet loaded with jewelry. We were like two kids in a candy store; instead of penny candy we waited patiently for our turn to select the most treasured piece of bling. Little did I know that this petite woman would become my mentor.

Skip forward a year in time and our love of shopping created the need for a place to sell our treasures. We made plans for our online shop called Lady Slippers, named after the wildflower and an Ojibwa Native American legend about a medicine man's wife named Koo-Koo-Lee. Growing up, Laureen had many teachers, one of whom was Native American. Laureen advised me that before we embarked on this new venture, I would be well served to do some work on myself as it would help build a strong foundation for our business. She said, "A house built on sand will not survive." Thus, following these Native American traditions, Laureen began to mentor me.

We set up and worked our on-line business in Laureen's living room. At three o'clock every day for over five years, Laureen and I would stop work and my lessons would begin over a cup of tea at her kitchen table. Her husband had lovingly coined these tea-time teachings Laureen's Boot Camp. In retrospect, from my vantage point today, given that her mentoring was spiritually based – I now refer to her sacred training as Laureen's Spiritual Boot Camp.

Laureen's one-on-one training involved different concepts every day. I was never told when to use this information, but to figure out for myself how to apply these concepts in my life. It was a challenge to complete my homework. Sometimes I was able to figure out my lessons right away; sometimes it took years and many lessons are to this day still a work in progress.

Life with Laureen was an adventure. One rainy day we went to the museum exhibit "A Day in Pompeii." As we turned into the parking garage entrance, a young Asian woman holding a large red umbrella walked in front of my car. I hit the brakes quickly, narrowly missing her. The woman continued on, oblivious to her newfound luck. I sat mesmerized, watching her red umbrella bob up and down as she walked away, then I continued into the parking garage.

I heard Laureen's voice in a perfect Mandarin dialect say "It's so dark in here." In shock, I glanced at Laureen, since Laureen did not speak Chinese. With no time to question her, I navigated the dark maze of the parking garage, leading us to the safety of a parking spot.

Upon exiting the car, Laureen said, "I was wondering why you looked at me in such confusion. I must have channeled that woman's grandmother." Suddenly it all made sense; it was that woman's grandmother who spoke through Laureen. We both burst into laughter. Awareness was a major point in Laureen's lessons and she showed me, in this instant, that messages can come from virtually anywhere and that I am not alone; guidance is always available if I just listen. The "unseen" and the "unspoken" can be recognized by opening up and paying attention.

The museum exhibit we visited that day was titled "A Day in Pompeii." We marveled at the homes and frescoes, the jewelry, and the gold coins. We came upon the back of the exhibit that housed the victims of the explosion. We walked somberly, each at opposite ends of the room, to where human victims were shown. Then both of us were drawn to the center of the room. A dog with a thick steel collar and long heavy chain was displayed in the contoured position in which he had died back in 79AD. Laureen said, "He never had a chance." I knew the dog died tethered to that chain. With heavy hearts, we both walked out of the museum. Laureen said that the gift of knowing is a double-edged sword. Together we experienced both edges of that blade.

It was this one-on-one mentoring by my friend and business partner that made me the person I am today. I graduated from Laureen's Spiritual Boot Camp. Because of her I am forever changed for the better. I strive to be in the moment, so that I can take time to listen, to feel, and make note of my surroundings; to learn the lessons that await my attention the first time around and therefore avoid learning them the hard way.

Laureen passed away nearly four years ago; however, even today I keep learning new concepts in Laureen's Spiritual Boot Camp. Believe me, she still doesn't give me a break nor does she accept my excuses as she has an even better view of my potential from her vantage point.

The Forgetting Garden
Annette Villaverde

It is grey inside: the walls, the ceiling, and the heaviness in the air like the sky before the storm. And this storm is brewing. I am waiting for the distant sound of thunder and lightning. After the lightning strikes, all that remains are ashes and broken bits. All those things happening outside of me, no control, just acceptance; that's the way it is. There is no real comfort from loss, from leaving behind everything familiar. How to cope with this? Forget to remember: a strategy I learned early on, no need to store my discomfort anywhere visible. Instead I send it deep down inside, making compost for my forgetting garden. I have rows of neatly tilled soil where all the hurt has been laid to rest. Nothing is visible in my garden. The soil is filled with sorrow, lack of self-worth, self-love, and self-care. There is no trust and no ability to communicate effectively, no place for these things above ground.

There is a pause in the storm, sweet like the dew in the morning sun, making everything appear magical, a spark of comfort, an unexpected kind gesture, the feeling of being heard, soft words, a smile, a feeling of inclusion. I have harvested from my forgetting garden, even though it appeared barren, all the magic brewing beneath the surface. Similar to the alchemy of carbon into diamonds, the process takes a long time, even given just the right amount of pressure, elements, inclusion of other material, and extreme heat. It is an uncomfortable process, yet it can't be done any other way. There are no shortcuts, no pieces to be left out. It is an exact recipe. It has its seasons and its cycles; its course is an adventure. Only when the process is complete can I see the beauty in it all.

As I look back I realize I could not be the person I am today without the pressures, the disruption, the intensity, and the changes. The result is compassion, the ability to love, to forgive, to see the innocence we all possess, and the possibility to grow no matter what adventures life brings. I may make a mistake, but looking back I see it was a needed part of the transformation for the highest good of all. My forgetting garden is producing more diamonds as I grow.

The Value of My Pain
Debra Bunszel

High School circa 1981. Missing the bus at my assigned stop, I ran the other direction to catch the second; *err, I hate my life*. That's me, pushing the limits to the very edge causing undue anxiety, stress, and chaos; thinking, *hey, I'm not good enough anyway and no one cares about me*, I rest in my seat. When I get to school, even though it is middle of Freshman year, I still cannot locate my locker, don't know its combination or my class schedule, what books I need or if I have done my homework. *Why do I feel bad, oblivious, and clueless as to the reason? Why isn't anyone helping me?* I don't know if anyone else lives this way.

Fast-forward a year or two. A school day ends and anxiety still rules my life. *Did I drive to school or take the bus? Why do my best friends have best friends?* I feel so lonely; even being class clown does not fill that void.

Further education, marriage, children, divorce, career, businesses, and all the luxury problems that go with a full life; I feel out of control. Even still, if there is no chaos I seem to cause it; I've always felt out of place otherwise. Feeling anxious I consider, *surely if I can control my environment, I will feel better about my circumstances.*

If I knew then what I know now, who would I be now? Fear cheated me from embracing that I don't have to be the person I was five minutes ago, even five seconds ago. So much suffering robbed me of being present, wanting to be and do something other than who and where I was. *Yes, let go of the control, you freak.* Downhearted, I asked my dad why I don't remember my life; his response, "Because you weren't there."

I could function if I stuffed my feelings, but I became numb, spiraling into physical and spiritual pain. I do not remember when alcohol first started to appease my low self-worth and give me the confidence that had been lost or never even fostered. Comparing my insides to others' outsides left me believing I was less than. My obsession would cause me to stumble through life for more than thirty years.

Then came the gift of desperation. I became willing to change. New fellowships and relationships started me on the path that was to lead me to me. Discovering and accepting my defects of character, uncovered through GOD's systematic way, I could now accept people and things. Happiness followed. My obsessions transformed to feelings, and my feelings became a sense of presence, guiding me to an unfamiliar way of life, one of seasons of self-discovery, gentle loving self-talk and heightened self-esteem.

I began to anchor more revelations into a new foundation, to empower and serve others. With this 20/20 hindsight, I found my worth, worth that was there all along. People started coming to me for help and healing, for my talents and gifts from GOD. Shining in GOD's Glory and Light, I found my purpose, one of Love, Honor, and Trust in Universal Life.

Weathering the Storm
Shaundale Rénà

It recently dawned on me that had one person said to me, "Girl, I've got you... If you need a place to stay; if you need to hold some cash; if you need me, I've got you," I would have left *seven years* ago. Seven years... Let that marinate.

Seven years is how long it's taken me to pay off bills, rebuild my credit, conceptualize a plan, and hear one of my closest friends say, "Girl, I know you. You're a planner. You will not do anything without a plan, and I know you're not going to move yourself or those kids without a way to maintain. We are buying a house next year, and if your plan hasn't come full circle before we do, you and those babies can come here." Sigh... That's exactly what I'd needed to hear... seven years ago.

Ending the call, I took several deep breaths. Breathe in... Breathe out... It soothed me, relaxed me... gave me something to hold on to. I took comfort in knowing someone knows the real me. Someone hadn't prejudged or condemned me according to their own standards because they recognized I have my own standards and that – bad or good, questionable or not – they're still mine. Someone gets me... now. Wait a minute, clearing my throat and popping the imaginary bubble dangling over my head... *Screeeeech! Braaaake! Haaaalt!* Let's back this wagon up and start at the beginning... seven years ago... at the beginning of the storm.

Have you ever felt like something wasn't right – no matter how you tried to convince yourself things would be okay, even when you didn't believe it yourself? Well, that's where I was. Something wasn't right, and no matter how hard I tried, I couldn't shake the feeling that something was coming I couldn't avoid.

I worried, I prayed, and then I finally got up the nerve to ask God to give me the strength to endure whatever this next season would bring… to show me what I was missing. Less than twenty-four hours later, He delivered. An e-mail from a stranger, a Facebook message from a second one… it was like chasing rabbits in a never-ending forest. I'm not going to lie to you… I lost it. And I did some things I will probably never write about either, as I'm sure many of you have had that moment when you knew, or you set your mind to finding out, then when you did… boom!

As you know, the confrontation is never fun. Well, let me back up again. Depending on which side of the playing field you're standing on, it very well might be a little entertaining. How can I say that, you ask? Because for me, it was very empowering to pick up the telephone and say, "May you someday achieve for yourself the life you so desperately hoped to acquire from me." Seriously, think about it. Suddenly, the hunter becomes the hunted. And, in this very instance, you can either have or lose everything.

I thought the storm was after my marriage. The howling winds and the pouring rains that followed…

the loud sounds of thunder and earthshattering clashes of lightening that ensued… I thought it all represented a struggle we were going through for God to do or give us something, perhaps even to take us somewhere. I believed that if I just held on a little longer and fought a little harder... if I just kept the faith and didn't give up, the sun would shine again. And I fought... I fought my man, I fought my marriage, I fought my Maker, and I fought myself. With each resistance, I bent – the harder the winds blew… the heavier the rains fell – until I collapsed.

In seasons of barrenness, you often believe you're not good enough to be, or do, or have anything. When my marriage didn't materialize the way I had envisioned, I finally came to realize I was the tree in the middle of the storm and it was not there to kill me; it wasn't there to break me; it was there to test me and to show me I was built to withstand. The blows that had come against me were intended to strengthen me, not to destroy me. I may have passed out, but I didn't die.

For years, exactly seven, I held onto a hope that – although real – was not mine. Like an umbrella turned inside-out, I had flipped. I took myself for granted and gave more to others than I did to myself. One day I got tired. I simply stopped. I stopped saying yes to everyone else, and boldly… confidently shouted YES to myself. I felt alive again. I did not feel guilty for not putting my kids first. I did not feel guilty for not giving in. I felt great. I felt so great I got my money in order, I got my life back in order, I started dreaming again and writing again. My vision is now my own. My kids will benefit, but they will not consume me. As for the marriage… well, as a result of weathering the storm I am now grounded. I walk with longer strides and respond with shorter answers. Because, what I know now that I didn't know then is: Once you prove to yourself you can make it, proving anything to anyone else is futile.

I'm Not Your Mistress
Margaret Brownlee

It was a typical Friday night in October, just one year after graduating from college. I was driving down Interstate 81 around 11:30 PM. It was my usual drive from Syracuse to Ithaca, New York.

The feeling of smooth black leather was cold under the palm of my hands. The taste of warm salty tears were streaming down my face, and the sight of a yellow faded line seemed to blur as I travelled miles upon miles down that two-way road.

"This is the last time I'm driving here," I said to myself in anger and frustration. I was actually fuming with anger. The palms of my hands started to sweat; my breathing became short and quick. I felt my right foot press so hard on the accelerator that my foot began to ache. My speed crept from 35 to 85 mph in seconds and I knew it was dangerous, but I didn't

171

care. All I wanted was to get away from her and all of those lies, secrets, and pain.

I shook my head in disbelief. "I can't believe I'm doing this again," I wanted to scream. I was so angry and disappointed. "Why? Why? Why? What is wrong with me?" I repeated this, three or four times, before coming out of my funk.

Ten minutes passed without my memory. It was difficult to see the road. The only thing that was keeping me focused were the lyrics to my favorite Ani DiFranco song "Untouchable Face." The most perfect lyric of that song was: *"F**k you for existing in the first place."*

F**k you! I am not your mistress. I don't like this feeling this way. I don't like being in this car; I don't want to be on this road. I hated her and her untouchable face. All I could think about was lighting another *American Spirit* cigarette and inhaling the sweet taste of cloves and nicotine, breathing in and out, and letting all of my problems fade away. Forget about it. She's not worth it. Everything is going to be okay. She doesn't love you. Take this moment as a life lesson and move on to bigger and better things. Fate is trying to teach you something. But why now?

Why this Friday night? Why now... when I'm alone and ashamed on this dark interstate road traveling by myself? I know this is wrong. I know that this isn't love. I know. I know. I know!

Had I known then what I know now I wouldn't have dated her in the first place. I wouldn't have looked her way. I wouldn't have let her charm and grace seduce me. I wouldn't have listened to her lies. I should have listened to my head and not my heart. She hurt me. She knew it.

It's been twelve years since I dated a married woman. She took advantage of my heart and soul. She didn't love me and she didn't care. It's not love when someone treats you as second-best. It's not love when someone lies to you and lies to themselves.

I know that now. My eyes are open. I know that I am perfect. I know that I am enough. I am not your mistress. I am powerful, beautiful, talented, and kind. All of my flaws were designed to make me the woman I am today, standing in front of you with shoulders strong, chin high and eyes bright. Note to self: You are amazing; don't ever forget that.

My Mother, My Champion
Vickie Martin-Conison

The day my brother and I laid my mother to rest, we watched as a thunderstorm was moving closer and closer. Thankfully, the rain held out until we got in the car, then the heavens opened. After several detours due to flooding, we finally arrived home safe and sound. Then the sun came out!

As I stood inside thinking about the last couple of years: my journey dealing with my mom and her dementia – a movement outside caught my eye. A beautiful red cardinal appeared outside the window, fluttering and begging for attention. Then another red cardinal appeared. I watched in amazement as the pair performed a beautiful dance, with me as the sole audience. When I walked to the window to get a closer look, I realized they were watching me, at which time they flew away. I knew then everything was going to be okay!

Even though moving my mother into hospice was a difficult decision, it was the right one. As I drove daily to visit her, I saw a mural on the side of a building with a painting of a cute puppy and the familiar quote, "Be the person your dog thinks you are." Knowing my mom always believed in me throughout my entire life and encouraged me to follow my own path, I finally realized I needed to be the person my mom believed me to be.

My mother had always been my champion. BUT, she wanted me to embrace the unique person she knew me to be. For instance, when I wanted to wear what everyone else was wearing, she would always say, "You will see yourself coming and going. You are the only YOU there is."

Whenever I made a mistake, she would repeatedly tell me that mistakes are always a lesson learned, and it is just as important to be as fair to myself as I am to others.

She repeatedly told me that it is okay to be different. She taught me if you spend your life trying to fit in, you run the risk of being overlooked. Fitting in is not only over-rated, it is boring. If you follow the crowd, chances are you will get lost.

Yes, she always encouraged me to find my path. And now I know how important it is to let go of what I think I "should" do. By following my heart more, I continually find what was meant to be.

Yes, everything is okay, and I continue to carry these precious memories with me.

Know Your Worth!
Theodora Sergiou

I was sixteen when my parents, brothers, and I decided to open a retail store. Young and relatively inexperienced in the retail pool industry, I was, however, a quick learner. As I stood behind the counter, customers who entered would ask for my father or brothers to help them. They did not believe a young girl had the knowledge or skills to be able to pull parts or advise them how to repair a pump or filter.

To earn the respect and confidence of my customers I needed to prove myself. So, I began to observe the cars as they parked. When I saw a customer holding a part in hand, I had their replacement part ready and waiting for them by the time they entered the store and arrived at the counter. Soon people began to trust my knowledge and experience. This helped me gain self-confidence.

After completing my education I moved overseas to Cyprus and then to England. The first year I lived in London, I was a happy tourist; the second year, I decided I needed to work. I interviewed and was immediately hired by an import/export company, with branches all over the UK, to help in two different departments. This was my first corporate job experience. The dress code dictated women were to wear only dresses or skirts, a far cry from my retail pool days!

In the mornings I worked in the buying department and afternoons were spent in the billing department. Having little to do in the afternoons, it became clear I was needed more in the mornings. I requested to be permanently placed in the buying department. After speaking with the department heads I was made an Assistant Buyer.

Proceeding to learn as much as I could, I was given increasingly important tasks with each passing week. One task was allocating stacks of import product requests from branches all over the country. I also sorted product requests to be transferred from one branch to another and decided how to divide each week's incoming shipments. The piles took up three tables full of stacks five to six feet tall. Fridays were spent looking over, sorting, and allocating the requests. The first Friday I began at 9:00 AM and completed the work at 11:00 PM.

Within a few weeks the piles were reduced to one small pile. I was the first person in years who took the time to look at each request, research branch stock levels, and then allocate each item to be delivered or transferred.

One day I went into work and was asked by the Director to join him in a meeting, and to bring in a pencil and pad. His secretary was out sick that day so I settled into my seat. He looked at me and suggested I ask the ten people in the room what they wanted to drink, write it down and go fetch their orders. I was humiliated. Not only was I not part of the meeting, I was asked to become a waitress.

Not wanting to be fired, I wrote down the orders and stepped outside the room. I went to my supervisor and told her what had happened; informing her I did not receive my MBA degree to become a waitress. After handing her the pad with the coffee and tea orders, I sat back down at my desk. She prepared the drinks and brought them to everyone in the meeting. I was never again asked to pick up a pencil and pad and join in. However, a few months later I was promoted.

Learning how to stand up for myself was daunting at times but needed to be done so as not to be "taken advantage of." There were several men in the office who were hired after me and had neither the qualifications nor position I held. Not one of them was asked to take drink orders. I learned to stand up for myself in order not to be discriminated against.

I believe women should learn from an early age to be bold and not be afraid to speak up when they are degraded or treated badly. So many times we back away and do as we are told, lacking the strength or courage to believe in ourselves, to stand up for ourselves.

Understanding that you are good enough, that you deserve the same respect and treatment as your colleagues from the onset is imperative. Demanding equal payment, equal opportunities, a safe working environment, and knowing your value is something that helps all women to believe in themselves and not accept ill treatment from anyone.

Having a good education, experience, and knowledge will ensure that a woman can be successful no matter the situation. Today, more than ever, it is important to stand up and be counted. I hope my experience helps women realize when a situation is not right you do not have to accept it. You are the master of your own destiny and must put things right by earning the respect of others and by knowing your worth.

The Burden of Regret
Lauren Langton

As I stand in the cold parking lot of the hospital waiting for my cousin, I feel hot anger boiling inside me. A civil war is raging between my father's family, and I have found myself on the front line. Within minutes of our conversation, I am hurling accusations and hurtful words at a person I once counted as one of my dearest friends. In that moment, despite my fury, I feel a deep pain of regret and overwhelming sorrow for all I have lost.

A few short years earlier our family was a strong, cohesive unit that would gather with love for more than just the holidays. Not to say it was a perfect Norman Rockwell family, but we shared true love and affection that seemed unbreakable. The demise of that happy family is a sordid tale. Tolstoy had it right when he said "Happy families are all alike; each unhappy family is unhappy in its own way."

It started with the shocking death of my uncle, Dennis. He was on his morning run when a heart attack ended his life far too early. I cannot recount with accuracy the harsh words and mistakes made after his death by all involved, and in truth, they're irrelevant now anyway. The results, however, I remember with vivid clarity. My grandfather's physical health declined and the chaos that ensued cost my grandmother her sanity in the most literal sense.

In the blink of an eye we had lost my uncle, my grandfather was deathly ill, and my grandmother was in a psychiatric ward in the throes of a psychotic break. I always thought tragedy brought a family together, and yet here I stood, unleashing blind rage on a dear friend turned enemy. Each trauma combined into a vortex, and we were all swept into a tornado of horror. As with any tornado, the debris left behind can never again reform to what it was. Such was the fate for us all. Siblings who once loved each other now could not be in the same room. Cousins who once played together refused to speak. Beloved grandparents who once held the family together were both essentially gone. Before these misfortunes I never dreamed such a loving family could turn on one another. This naivety left me ill prepared for the monumental suffering that was to follow.

I have learned, and continue to learn countless lessons from this devastating collapse. However, one lesson has changed my life for the better and has allowed me to derive some gratitude from the experience. The realization came from the teachings of Achaan Chaa, a Thai meditation master instrumental in bringing Therevada Buddhism to the west. He spoke of his favorite goblet. When tapped, this material possession brought him great joy with its pleasing patterns and pleasant ring. Yet he knew its fragile nature would someday cause it to break and so he looked upon it as if it were already gone. This very simple lesson took root deep inside me.

I began to look at all of my earthly possessions and my relationships as if they were already broken. An entirely predictable thing happened: I became grateful for every second spent with those I cherish, in a way I never had before. The agony of grief is incapacitating enough without the added burden of regret. My new perspective became the ultimate prevention to that added burden.

In the decade after this painful ordeal, I spent the first week of October at a camping compound my great uncle, Matt, created. He was my grandfather's brother, and in many ways, became a surrogate for him after he passed. Matt was the type of person who collected a following by being his genuine, loving self; people drove from as far away as Mexico and Kentucky all the way to Northern Maine to share his company. The only difference in their adoration from mine was my newfound determination to prevent regret. Each year I would hug my great uncle as if he was already gone. I memorized the family stories he shared as if I would never have the chance to hear them again. I never missed a chance to share how deeply I treasured our time together and the knowledge he shared with me.

Unsurprisingly, when his inevitable death came I could not escape the grief. Yet, for the first time in my life I was not burdened with a single regret – truly. I searched as deep as my mind could go and no hint of remorse could be found. No words were left unspoken and no moment taken for granted.

As I write this my three dogs lie beside my feet. They are young and healthy, hopefully with long lives ahead of them, yet I know they are already gone. Due to this knowing, I cannot muster much anger when they eat an expensive shoe or jump onto the couch covered in mud. I play with them outside just a bit longer despite the cold air or rain. The sum of these minor behavioral changes will soften the blow when they cross the Rainbow Bridge and are gone from my lap forevermore.

This lesson in regret was hard learned and yet it has given me a truly invaluable gift: true appreciation for my life and for those with whom I am blessed to share it.

My Fearless Five-Year-Old Self
Karen Leeds

At age five, I led exercises for the whole school. Clearly, I was born to be a leader! But then I noticed my mother felt uncomfortable being the center of attention. That started me questioning my boldness. On top of that, a series of events every two years had me become painfully shy.

We moved across the country when I was six. At my new school I felt awkward among strangers – preferring to know people I encountered. I didn't like feeling anonymous.

When I was eight years old, I remember a guy calling out to me, "Did you use an eggbeater on your hair?" His teasing made me withdraw further. I guess sometimes being anonymous is better. My mom started making me scrambled eggs after school to comfort me.

One day, when I was ten, I walked home from school to discover my next-door neighbor sitting on her lawn with two girlfriends; I recognized one of them, Tessa, from school. Deciding this was a great opportunity to be social, I walked over and said hi to them. Tessa casually informed me that I was not welcome there. Then she spat at me! I was in shock. Before I could respond, the other two followed her lead. Embarrassed, I slowly walked away, but maintained eye contact to show I wasn't going to be intimidated. I felt like an outsider. How unfair. What had I done? Why was she so mean to me? No amount of scrambled eggs would help.

A few months later, Tessa was hanging upside down from the parallel bars at school and fell. She was screaming in pain. I didn't want to help her – she had spat on me. But school was over and there was nobody else around. I couldn't in good conscience ignore her, could I? After debating with myself about it, I decided to get help. I hoped that if it had happened to me, she too, would have gotten an adult.

Tessa came to school the next day in two casts that were crossed, held up by slings and taped to her body, across her chest. She had broken both arms, was helpless, and refused to look at me. I felt sad for her in a way, but she had treated me very badly. I guess karma can be a bitch.

At age twelve, I went to the mall and bought a typical "sixties" mini-skirt polyester romper: bright orange-red with white polka dots. The outfit also included a separate skirt which you could decide to wear, or not. I was so excited – I looked like a model. I had definitely never felt so cool and sexy. This was going to turn things around. The next day I wore it to school. After lunch, I decided to modify the outfit and instead wear the skirt as a cape. Feeling invincible and all-powerful, I had emerged from my shell. My transformation to super hero was complete! But then, a kid noticed and very loudly said "Hey, weren't you wearing that as a skirt earlier?" I melted into an introverted puddle... back to my scrambled eggs comfort food.

At age fourteen, I was in the dance chorus for a musical. This was quite a stretch for painfully shy me. When they put makeup and a wig on me nobody knew who I was. I was a bit surprised, but I had kept to myself and hadn't talked to very many students. They were all whispering, "Who is that?" Apparently during rehearsals, I had been so quiet I was completely forgettable! I just smiled – let them guess who I might be!

Throughout most of my life I lacked the confidence to put myself out there. As a people pleaser, my focus was definitely on other people at my own expense. I was jealous of others who felt comfortable in front of a crowd. They weren't self-conscious at all. How did that happen? Why couldn't I be like that? What was wrong with me? Why couldn't I go back to feeling fearless like I was at age five?

After decades of reading personal growth books and attending many courses, I finally gave myself permission to just be my fearless five-year-old self again.

Bottom line: Who I am is good enough. And if others don't like or appreciate me, TOUGH. Frankly their opinion is really none of my business anyway.

I'm the same person I was, though society has tried to mold me into a widely accepted, watered-down version of me. Enough of that nonsense – I suppose age also has something to do with my changing. At some point, I decided if I'm okay with me, it's less of a concern that others might want me to conform. After all, my unlikely cartoon hero, Popeye, said, "I yam what I yam."

So, do yourself a favor – be fully YOU – no excuses – no hiding – no waiting for the right time. Do it now. Worry less about others. Stop trying to keep up the image you think society wants. It's actually much simpler to just be yourself, be present, and not judge yourself against some impossible standard: no awkwardness, nasty hair comments, spitting episodes, skirt to cape fiascos or innocent bystander conscience-testing required!

No Reward in Playing Small
Kimberly Broome

Hello, my name is Kim and I am a food addict.

I believe our struggles in life are all in preparation for our calling. I mean, how else can you explain a former binger and overeater becoming a successful weight loss coach?

As a kid who hated school and whose parents both worked, I would come home to an empty house and fill my time by watching TV, drinking soda, and eating potato chips and Chips Ahoy cookies. My bad food habits may have started off as a convenient snack – but they soon turned into a source of comfort and numbing during a couple of rough years as a kid. I'm talking a young kid – six to seven years old, the formative years – and man, those habits run deep!

I can remember when I started to recognize these same patterns within myself as an adult. I became aware that on the nights I came home to an empty house – I would find myself wandering around the kitchen aimlessly, back and forth from the TV to the cupboards to the fridge, obsessively snacking – same pattern as when I was a kid.

Food had always been my drug of choice.

Taking back control was a great triumph for me, realizing the power of the food I was putting in my body – good or bad. When I eat "good" – I feel "good"! When I feel "good" – I do "good"! I am alert, productive, and pleasant. When I eat like "crap" – I feel like "crap." I am unmotivated; I think negatively and can be downright unpleasant to be around.

Simple really, but I know it's not easy, as every now and again the familiar patterns would resurface.

A friend and business partner of mine suggested coaching to me. She knew how much I loved nutrition and fitness. I mean, "Hell," from the age of ten I had been reading every diet book and magazine that I could put my hands on. I loved the idea (in theory)! Problem was I didn't have the confidence; I thought I needed to be PERFECT. While I was fit and in shape, I knew my demons and struggles and worried it could all change "on a dime." I flat-out doubted my ability to help others.

It took me years to move forward and act on this vision. Thank God my friend believed in me more than I did! "Funny" how she could see the potential in me that I just couldn't see for myself. I guess that's what I love about what I do – I get to pay it forward.

Realizing I had the ability to help others on their journey was profound for me. Finding the courage to put myself out there as a coach has been one of the most rewarding experiences in my life. It has opened so many new opportunities for me. I have assisted in some amazing life transformations. It's not just about the weight – it's about the energy and light my clients bring to the world when they are showing up for themselves. I've seen women take control of their health then go on to launch amazing new projects and businesses. I've seen them empowered to set a new standard in their household and become a shining example for their children and spouse. I've seen them do things they would never have taken a step toward had they not been feeling their very best.

Each new level of growth as an entrepreneur has required me to look deeper within myself. It has not always been easy. Being SEEN and HEARD was uncomfortable for me and has required me to really dig deep. (HA! You probably wouldn't have guessed that by looking at my Facebook page today!) Thing is, I know that in order to make a bigger impact I need to allow myself to be seen and to be vulnerable.

Growing my coaching practice has enabled me to reflect back on that insecure person and understand the journey thus far. It has allowed me to acknowledge how I used food to cope with things that were going on in my life.

And boy, if I could go back – I would know how much stronger I really was, both as a kid and an adult. I wouldn't have wasted all those years playing small. I would have stepped up sooner.

That thing inside you, the voice that says you are meant for more, that you can do better, that you have more to give: that is not a wish or a dream. It is your God-given talent. Honor it, respect it, and nurture it. Let it out!

We cannot let ourselves be defeated. We need to overcome and triumph. There is no reward in playing small. It serves nobody. We are here to push through and shine our light so others can shine theirs.

My Own Best Friend
Jessica Boelte

Over decades of life experiences worthy of therapy, and the occasional trauma thrown in for color, I had come to base my value/worth on the approval of other people and the love of a significant other. If I didn't have both, or God forbid neither, I told myself I was "not worthy," "not enough," "inherently flawed," and "unlovable." It became so engrained in my mind that being alone was almost unbearable. I just needed so badly to feel worthy. I realize now that what I needed was to recognize my own value, to stop being my own worst enemy and instead be my OWN best friend and advocate.

I wish I had known then that by being my own worst enemy, I made every negative experience ten times worse than it ever would have been on its own, and that had I been my own best friend, I would have recovered more quickly and learned from those experiences. Instead, I told myself lies. I told myself my needs weren't important. I told myself that it was selfish to ask for help. I told myself that I would be alone if I set boundaries. I told myself that no one would ever love me just the way I am. Then, instead of being angry with people who hurt me, I blamed myself. I told myself it was because I was _____ (naïve, stupid, ugly, fat, insecure, pathetic… pick a negative adjective).

Even as I began to recognize that I deserved better, instead of showing myself compassion for dealing with life in the best way I knew how, I was angry with myself for not being more kind to Jessica. I was angry at myself for not taking better care of her, for not respecting her wishes, for compromising her values, for risking her long-term health, for not taking her future into consideration, for not chasing her dreams. I was angry at myself for allowing her to be mistreated, for choosing to numb and ignore her pain rather than let her heal, for not letting her be exactly who she was born to be, for demanding perfection from her, for criticizing her every time she fell short of it, for making HER feel guilty for being taken advantage of, beaten, and even raped.

In a small group counseling session one day, someone interrupted me trying to "rescue" someone else and told me that I mattered too. He told me that my needs and desires were just as important as anyone else's. As an exercise, he made one of those plastic pin-on name tags that said "I MATTER" for me to wear. I wore it and everywhere I went, people, even strangers, said "Yeah! You do matter" and smiled at me. He challenged me to wear it until I FELT it, BELIEVED it. I wore that silly, handmade name tag for five days and then I gave it someone else I met who needed to hear it as much as I had.

This prompted me to print about one hundred bumper stickers that said "YOU MATTER," and I gave them to friends and family, the grocery store cashier, the gas station attendant, at drive-through windows and to my kids' friends. I had a bunch left over, so I posted them in groups on Facebook and offered to mail them for free. The response was overwhelming. It went viral and international in days. So, I ordered more... and then more... and then more. I shared what a blessing it had been for me, to hand stickers to total strangers, at just the moment when their day could not get worse, to see their eyes well with tears as they thanked me and hugged me. "How did you know?" they would ask.

Today, as of this writing, I have printed and distributed 3,500 stickers in fourteen different countries.

I am finally learning to accept and love myself; learning that what others think of me has absolutely no bearing on who I am or who I'm supposed to be. I am treating myself with the same unconditional love, devotion, and protection I give others. I know that, I too, deserve to be happy. I MATTER! My life is precious. I am worthy of love, respect, and affection. I give myself permission to say no, permission to set boundaries, and permission to seek out and pursue the things that bring me joy. Caring for myself is not self-indulgent. It is an act of survival.

There are people who would take advantage of me, if I let them, leaving me feeling unlovable and "fortunate" that they stay with me. And while painful, sometimes the "familiar" feels safer than to leap without a net towards what I know in my heart I desire but am afraid to believe I deserve. That choice is MY responsibility. Psychology tells us, "We seek out what we know." My experience has been that I attached myself to those very much like the person who made me feel "less than" in the first place.

I hate saying this and I have to remind myself every day. But we have to love ourselves enough to walk away from those who hurt us and set boundaries, to protect ourselves from those who would seek to do the same in our futures.

Stop being your own worst enemy. It's time to be your own best friend. YOU MATTER!!!

Benz's Last Ride
Annette LeCompte

I was just finishing up at the barn the other day when I heard Lisa call out "Hey Annette, come here. You have to ride Benz before he leaves – you've never sat on him!" It was the weekend before Benz was being sent to upstate NY to retire. He used to be a race horse and quite a good one. He was a money maker so he had raced until he was seven; and at eighteen, those hard miles were beginning to take their toll. Lisa had owned him since he came off the track, and loved him dearly, even though he wasn't always easy to love. Off-the-track thoroughbreds are high spirted, sensitive, and prone to acting out. She joked that he was the hot-looking bad boy that you shouldn't date, but you just couldn't help yourself.

There was a reason I had never ridden him. I had always played it safe, which isn't always a bad thing when it comes to horses. As a kid, my parents sent me for lessons off and on, but compared to other girls I felt awkward and ignorant, a terminal intermediate. Nevertheless, I continued to cherish the dream of having a horse of my own.

I was thirty when I bought Jay, and the learning curve was steep. He was inexperienced, as was I. If there was a stupid thing to do on or around a horse I pretty much did it, and in full view of everyone at the barn. Against all the odds, though, we managed to do things together I never dreamed possible. He was the storybook horse you read about – the one who loves his rider and is always doing something smart and brave to save the day. I gave him all the credit he deserved, happily resigned to the fact that I wasn't in the same league as the other woman at the barn. I didn't jump big jumps, I didn't go to horse shows, and I was intimidated by hot, sensitive horses like Benz. Yet the instant Lisa asked me to jump on I knew I had to. It would somehow help her to say goodbye if I shared that last ride.

Gingerly, I mounted Benz, still a bit unsure. Much to my surprise, we conversed easily and elegantly through the subtle pressure of legs and hand. Someone called out "Look how pretty Benz looks!" and I felt a surge of pride. I told Lisa "I can't believe he's being so good for me!" She answered, "That's because he knows you get it, Annette; he respects you." My heart was filled with wonder and sadness.

Wonder for the gift Benz had given me and sadness for what could have been – what we could have shared, what he could have taught me, what I should have known. I had done us both a disservice. Benz, the difficult, fractious racehorse had given me the respect I never gave to myself. In that moment I wished that I had long ago shed the image of the "struggling wannabe rider" I had been, and embraced the horsewoman I had become.

OUR BIOGRAPHIES

Nancy K. Armstrong

Nancy overcame a difficult childhood and many hardships to become the strong, powerful, and inspirational woman she is today: a hard-working single mother, raising her child with an open heart and thoughtful mind. Standing strong in her truth, she visualizes greatness and motivates others to do the same.

• Page 89 •

Jennifer Bingham-Maas

Jennifer, a mother of three teenagers and the wife of Norm, is an avid reader and a dabbler in writing. She pursues her love of language through her work as a pediatric speech-language pathologist helping infants and toddlers learn to better communicate.

• Page 11 •

Melissa Bloodgood

Almost thirty, Melissa has created a quiet life in the suburbs of Boston. She lives with her fiancé and his two daughters, along with their two dogs in a little house next to the public library. They do not have a TV and rather like it that way.

• Page 95 •

Jessica Boelte

Jessica holds an MBA and worked in IT until choosing to become a stay-at-home mother. Since then, she has acquired six fitness certifications, placed second in her first Women's Figure competition, and now runs her own business, Healthy Self Images. Jessica is passionate about helping others learn to love themselves.

• Page 201 •

Stephanie Borden

Stephanie is a helper. As the owner of her own personal concierge services business, she is dedicated to helping her clients improve their quality of life. After raising three children and spending over thirty years in corporate banking, she has learned how to face fear and successfully move forward.

• Page 37 •

Kimberly Broome

Kimberly is a certified weight loss coach specializing in inflammation, hormone imbalance, and hidden food intolerances. Kim has helped hundreds of women lose significant weight and inches. Most important, she has helped them to transform their lives and reclaim their confidence with the use of proper nutrition.
www.KimberlyBroome.com

• Page 197 •

Margaret Brownlee

Margaret is a working professional, a mom, and loving wife. She has a Master's degree in Education and a Bachelor's degree in Theater. Margaret hopes her story will inspire others to love themselves and believe that they are enough.

• Page 171 •

Debra Bunszel

Debra is a Reflexologist, Reiki Master, Organizer and SoulCollage® facilitator embracing her talents through teaching Introduction to Reflexology, Mom-Me Take Your Shoes Off, and all levels of Reiki in groups and personal sessions, as well as collage-making through essence of one's core: "Touching the soul of the sole."
www.TouchTheSole@aol.com

• Page 161 •

Kelley Cabral-Mosher

Kelley Cabral-Mosher, LICSW, owns Freedom Wellness & Counseling where healing and recovery are the foundation of her work. Kelley lives in New Bedford, Massachusetts, with her husband, two sons, and dog. She loves her family and friends, exercising, practicing yoga, meditation and mindfulness, and coaching Girls basketball and field hockey.

• Page 7 •

Loba Chudak

Loba is a life balance coach and soul vision mentor. She supports motivated women to nurture their innate wisdom and creative potential, so they can follow and express their heart's desire with vitality and consequence. A practicing artist and musician, she lives with her husband in Champaign, Illinois. www.LobaChudak.com

• Page 51 •

Nell Conway

Nell received her degree in Arts Management from Virginia Commonwealth University, which led her to work in the hospitality industry for over a decade while traveling the world. She is now a freelance event coordinator.

• Page 17 •

Deborah Corrigan

A native New Englander, Debbie is married and an entrepreneur. Her online shop, Lady Slippers, makes a difference in this world by giving back to charities and sparking new life in unwanted vintage and antique items. Every day is an adventure in her search to uncover the next hidden treasure. www.Lady-Slippers.com

• Page 151 •

Diane Marie Ford

Certified Holistic Counselor, Spirit Medium, author of *The Spirits Speak on Success*, Diane teaches women how to become the best damn version of themselves with guidance from their ancestors. She lives with her wife, two dogs, several rescued cats, a flock of hens, and one handsome rooster in southeastern Massachusetts.

• Page 31 •

Laura Fry

Laura is a full-time engineer, as well as an investor and inventor. She has published her first children's book titled *Mama's New Friend*. Laura lives with her daughter in Phoenix, Arizona.

• Page 85 •

Katharine Gilpin

Katharine's Drama BA from Tufts University, theatre production career, and decades as a bodywork therapist, reflect her passion for helping others to feel their "Bravo!" A native New Yorker – Massachusetts is now her home. Katharine enjoys watching foreign films and spending time with her wife and household of companion critters.

• Page 135 •

Enna Jimenez

Enna is VP, Quality Engineering Director at Eastern Bank with over 25 years in the field. She is President of Association of Latino Professionals for America (ALPFA), Boston Chapter. Enna sits on the boards MA Latino Advisory Commission, MA Commonwealth Corporation, Beaver Country Day School, and Hyde Square Task Force.

• Page 27 •

Lauren Langton

Lauren lives in Massachusetts with her husband, Mathew. She works for BNI, a networking organization that helps people build their business through the philosophy of Givers Gain©. They have three precious dogs and dream of starting a dog rescue. She believes that with positivity and perseverance all things are possible.

• Page 185 •

Lau Lapides

Lau is President of Lau Lapides Company, training professional actors in voice overs and broadcasting for radio, television, and film. Her awards include Women Who Make a Difference, 100 Women We Admire, and The Imaginaire Award for Excellence in Broadcasting/Entertainment. Lau has been featured in *Backstage* and *Imagine* magazines.

• Page 41 •

221

Annette LeCompte

Annette is a businesswoman, entrepreneur, and an avid equestrian who deeply believes in the healing power of horses. She hopes her story will encourage other woman to stop viewing who they are through the lens of who they were.

• Page 207 •

Stephanie Lee

Stephanie is a group fitness instructor and massage therapist practicing in the San Diego area. She teaches a variety of fitness formats and loves to help her students have fun while working out. www.stephaniealee.com

• Page 1 •

Karen Leeds

Karen, founder of Life Coaching Magic, helps people bring their dreams to earth. Her book, *Life's Magic Carousel: How to Grab the Brass Ring Before the Music Stops,* is soon to be published. She has written thirteen articles for The Good Men Project; these apply to women too.

www.LifeCoachingMagic.com

• Page 191 •

Lauren Lemieux

Lauren chose to leave her family's business after eighteen years to find her true purpose. She is now an ICF-accredited certified life coach (CTI). Her clients are both private individuals looking for personal fulfillment and small business owners striving for professional success.

www.LaurenLemieux.com

• Page 147 •

Alina Lopez-Thomas

Alina earned her undergraduate degree in Business Management and a Business Planning certificate. She has thorough knowledge of compliance in the fields of Child Care and Early Education. Alina formed *The Greater Resource of Women Networks* (GROWN) in 2016 to empower aspiring business-minded women with practical skills and coaching for success.

• Page 71 •

Dawna McCarthy Cannon

Dawna is a professional Travel Consultant. Along with her husband, they have a merged family of three children, their spouses, and six grandchildren. She is a seeker of knowledge and experiences. Dawna loves to explore the world, both physically and via the web, to enhance and perpetuate her spiritual growth.

• Page 47 •

Heather McCarthy

Heather is a dedicated single mom to her wonderful daughter, Caroline. She dreams of one day owning a home with a workshop, so she can get lost in her projects. She wants other women to know they are not alone in their pain although often it may feel that way.

• Page 115 •

Tara McKenzie Gilvar

Tara has decades of experience building some of the nation's most highly desired consumer brands. Her vast branding and marketing experience helped her launch the popular women's empowerment and entrepreneur organization B.I.G., which is dedicated to helping women live the lives they are meant to live. www.BelieveInspireGrow.com

• Page 67 •

Vickie Martin-Conison

Vickie is a native Atlantan, currently residing in Decatur, Georgia, with her photographer husband and three dogs. Her corporate career was in advertising, but that ended in 2015. At that time, she began pursuing art full-time and leading workshops in the Atlanta area.

• Page 175 •

Michele Medeiros

Michelle learned how to quilt in high school Home Economics class. When she needed a career change, Michelle decided to go for it and open her own quilt store so area quilters would have a place to go to buy great fabric, and collaborate. www.homesteadquiltingandfabrics.com

• Page 121 •

Melissa Murphy

Melissa is co-founder of Insight of Success, LLC and a certified speaker, coach and teacher. She empowers individuals and organizations in their personal and professional development. Melissa's work covers a global footprint sharing the value of **R**elationships, **E**quipping, **A**ttitude, **L**eadership, and **C**larity. Melissa loves inspiring others to live fully. www.insightofsuccessllc.com
• Page 75 •

Deborah O'Brien

Deborah, author of *Bliss: Behind the Mask,* is an inspirational speaker, teacher, and founder of Bliss Full, a self-image consulting company. She helps liberate women from destructive patterns and limiting beliefs via an eight-stage process that healed her life twenty-six years ago after a near-death encounter. www.deborahobrienbliss.com
• Page 57 •

Nancy O'Keefe

Nancy O'Keefe, MBA, is a strategic adviser, executive coach, speaker, trainer and author. She works with business owners and senior executives to create profitable, productive workplaces, helping them attract, motivate, and retain great people. She is a thought leader around management and employees. www.NancyOKeefeCoaching.com.
• Page 79 •

Maura O'Leary

Maura is a successful business executive whose career motto is "Live Fearlessly!" She recently focused her goals on writing and has published a book, *When Angels Play Poker* – a lifetime dream! She hopes to inspire others through her enclosed story. Maura lives in the Boston, Massachusetts, area.
• Page 63 •

Sheila Pearl

Author and Relationship Coach Sheila Pearl has been to the top of the mountain, living her dream as an opera singer, cantor, psychotherapist, and teacher. At age seventy-six, she is The Love Doctor of the Hudson Valley, helping her clients to create and maintain loving relationships. www.SheilaPearl.com

• Page 105 •

Katrina Piehler

Katrina is a wellness coach who is passionate about helping busy women to breathe new energy into their lives. The heart of her work is about learning to live powerfully from the inside, out. You can learn more about her offerings at www.Living-from-Center.com

• Page 111 •

Shaundale Rénà

Shaundale is a writer, a speaker, and an inspirational teacher who seeks to empower those in transition through colorful stories of desperation and contempt. She is the author of the 2016 Chrystal Award-winning upcoming release, *Second Time Around*. Her interests include reading (anything), writing (anytime), and traveling (anywhere). www.Wattpad.com/StonyRhodes
• Page 165 •

Tina Sarcia-Maxwell

Tina, owner of Inner Wellness, is a passionate Certified Holistic Health Coach. She journeys with her clients to honor their health goals, offering one-on-one support and guidance to promote a fulfilling life for the mind, body, and soul. www.InnerWellness.optavia.com
• Page 125 •

Theodora Sergiou

As President of Nicholas Pools Incorporated, Theodora has been awarded Top 25 Leading Woman Entrepreneur from *NJ Monthly* magazine, Brava Award from *Smart CEO* magazine, and Woman of Distinction Award from Professional Women in Construction. She holds an MBA from Rider University and a BSc. from Georgian Court University.

• Page 179 •

Lisa Sinkiewicz

As a beloved child of God, Lisa is healing and thankful for the process. She is a survivor, but that is only part of her story. She feels blessed to be living life with her husband and children, learning each day and loving each moment together.

• Page 21 •

Lisa Sullivan Bond

Lisa has worked for NGOs, promoted Solar Energy with nonprofits, USDOE, volunteered in schools, and social agencies. Proud of her daughter: art teacher and mother of an adorable two-year-old; and her son: mental health counselor; and her two stepdaughters and their families. Interests: travel, sports, and supporting social justice.

• Page 99 •

Wendy Tayer, PhD

A UCSD faculty member and licensed clinical psychologist, Wendy is married with three children, ages eighteen, twenty-two and twenty-five. She enjoys walking her dog, water aerobics, gyrotonics, cooking, hiking, girls' trips, and world travel. Dr. Tayer, founder of a community book club, is a CERT member, writer, lecturer and community volunteer.

• Page 141 •

Annette Villaverde

Annette is a mother, partner, life coach, yoga instructor, essential oil educator, and a consummate learner. She defines life success by how many lives she has improved, inspired, or touched in a meaningful way. The greatest gift Annette shares is helping to empower you to live a life you love.

• Page 157 •

Lena Winston

Lena is a retired pediatric occupational therapist, and is now a stay-at-home mom with three daughters: ages twenty-five, twelve, and ten. She lives in Hamilton, Massachusetts, with her husband, children, and two dogs. Lena loves nature, animals, spirituality, and raw food cooking and sprouting.

• Page 131•

CONTRIBUTOR INDEX

Each contributing writer is listed in alphabetical order by last name with the page number of the beginning of her story.

ACKNOWLEDGEMENTS

Our sincerest gratitude is given to Dana Schomp, who, from the very onset, encouraged us to develop our seed concept of In Your Own Words Women through the production of this book. She held the space for us to feel the breadth and power of this collaborative creation.

A multitude of thanks to contributor Stephanie Lee, whose unflagging belief in this book project propelled us forward. The first woman to show up and voice her desire to "be a part of" by writing her story, she wholeheartedly stepped up, cheered us on, spread the word, and referred many women to join in and express themselves through the power of the written word.

"Thank you!" to Ellen Wanamaker, who made herself, along with her website expertise, available as we ran into challenges building the website. Her positive can-do attitude was indeed a Godsend.

"Bravo!" to Tara McKenzie Gilvar and Nell Conway who added the B.I.G. element by facilitating virtual interviews and press to promote us within the *Believe Inspire Grow* community.

We offer immense gratitude to the indefatigable Grammar Goddess, our copy editor, Susan Rooks, who made the editing process seem effortless. Our communications were educational, animated, and invigorating. Thanks also go to Sarah Holroyd for her patience and skill in bringing our book cover to life.

There would be no book without the willingness, support, patience, and creativity of every writer who believed in herself, and us, enough to take a chance and dive into the process. From the depth of our hearts to the height of our visions, we applaud this community of creative women in celebration of our individual and collective accomplishments. We hold dear and honor the numerous and magical newfound connections.

PUBLISHER'S NOTE

The views presented in this book do not necessarily reflect those of the publisher, which accepts no responsibility for inaccurate information or for each individual contributor's viewpoint. All the information in this book is published in good faith and for general information purposes only. We make no warranties about the completeness, reliability and accuracy of this information.

Any action you take upon the information in this book is strictly at your own risk. The publisher is not liable for any losses or damages in connection with your use of the content herein. We do not dispense medical advice or prescribe any technique as a form of treatment for physical, emotional, or medical problems without the advice of a physician, either directly or indirectly. Our intent is only to offer information of a general nature to help you in your quest for emotional and spiritual well-being. In the event you use any of the information in this book for yourself, which is your constitutional right, we, the publishers, Katharine Gilpin and Diane Marie Ford, assume no responsibility for your action. If you need support, please seek the help of a professional.

movie "Puzzle"
Fascism: A Warning—
Madeleine Albright

Made in the USA
Middletown, DE
19 July 2018